Thrive

Thrive

Six Key Principles for Wildly Successful Business

*Your Business Mastery Playbook:
Creating Financial Freedom through Business*

Lincoln **Pan**

Copyright © 2019 by Lincoln Pan.

Library of Congress Control Number:		2019902331
ISBN:	Hardcover	978-1-7960-0114-3
	Softcover	978-1-7960-0113-6
	eBook	978-1-7960-0112-9

All rights reserved. No part of this book may be reproduced or transmitted in any form or by any means, electronic or mechanical, including photocopying, recording, or by any information storage and retrieval system, without permission in writing from the copyright owner.

Any people depicted in stock imagery provided by Getty Images are models, and such images are being used for illustrative purposes only.
Certain stock imagery © Getty Images.

Print information available on the last page.

Rev. date: 02/27/2019

To order additional copies of this book, contact:
Xlibris
1-800-455-039
www.Xlibris.com.au
Orders@Xlibris.com.au
789059

CONTENTS

Praise For vii
Acknowledgements.. xi
Introduction xv
    Who Is Lincoln? And Why Did He Write This Book? xv
    Why Read *Thrive?* xxi

CHAPTER ONE
Principle 1: Transform Your Mindset 1
    Distinction #1: Four Sources of Income, Not All Paths
    Are Created Equal 8
    Distinction #2: You Get Paid for the Value You Create,
    Not Your Time 18
    Distinction #3: Transformed from Consumer to
    Producer, Business is One of the Fastest Vehicles to
    Create Value and Increase Your Income 20

CHAPTER TWO
Principle 2: Hustle Your Way Up 24
    The Need to Focus on Your One Thing 29
    Business and Financial Success Are Forged by Process,
    Not by Events 36

CHAPTER THREE
Principle 3: Recognise Your Strength 41
    Distinction #1: Pain + Reflection = Progress 42
    Distinction #2: Artist + Operator + Manager =
    Well-Designed Business 46

    Distinction #3: Business Mastery ≠ Artist Mastery ≠ Technical Skills Mastery 49
    Distinction #4: Three Business Development Stages.............53

CHAPTER FOUR
Principle 4: Improvise. Adapt. Overcome. 61
    Distinction #1: Design Your Way to Success......................63
    Distinction #2: Align Your Passion with Your Business.........73

CHAPTER FIVE
Principle 5: Visualise the Compelling Future 80
    Distinction #1: How to Turn Nothing into Something 83
    Distinction #2: Begin with Why 90
    Distinction #3: Your Business Is the Way to More Life.........95

CHAPTER SIX
Principle 6: Empower Your Team..100
    Distinction #1: How Situations Occur to Team = Team Performance 106
    Distinction #2: Future-Based Language Elevates Team Performance 110
    Distinction #3: Trade Your Expectation for Appreciation 114

Now It Is Your Time 119
Further Reading... 121
About the author... 123
Index... 125

Praise For

Thrive: Six key principles for wildly successful business

As a business minded person and someone that is always interested to self-improvement I can highly recommend this book to anyone that wants to transform their business or improve their life skills in general. Lincoln truly captured the essence of his business and life success in this book that will provide great value and insight to you, no matter if you are a student or an executive.

Sebastian Lang
Management Consultant
McKinsey & Company

THRIVE is an alchemy of knowledge, books, insights, experience, personal transformation and wisdom. From Confucius to Cash Flow Quadrants, it captures the author's authentic recollection of life lessons, reflected upon through a myriad of models and frameworks. One of the central tenants of the book is change vs transformation; the key distinction here is that the latter is internal.

As you navigate the book through the six key principles you can't help but find yourself as a candid observer of the spiritual journey of Lincoln's Self that culminated at the apex of Maslow's hierarchy, self-actualization. The words are intentional and are masterfully captured in a language designed to inspire, excite and stimulate the reader.

The author's authenticity in recollecting his personal dilemmas throughout his journey helps connect the reader with his humanity. You are present to Lincoln's courage and compassion as he captures value from life only to create it in the form of a blueprint for financial freedom.

Lincoln's ability to simplify and amalgamate multiple concepts and apply systemic thought processes such as design thinking to the actual generation of the book in itself is impressive and artful.

THRIVE is indeed an inspiringly distinct creation by an extraordinary individual.

Krish Vallipuram
Change & Communications Consultant
RAC

By sharing his relevant experiences and opportunities for personal and business improvement, Lincoln has reignited the energy within myself. I look forward to using this book as one of my many strategies for not only achieving more, but to prosper and THRIVE in the future that I am the creator of.

Peter Siwek

Subsea Project Engineer, TechnipFMC

"THRIVE is like a magical manifesto for manifesting meaning and money.

And no one better than Lincoln to create this scintillating manual for achieving personal satisfaction and professional greatness.

As a co-learner on the MBA journey, I have personally witnessed Lincoln 'walk the talk' on the six time-tested principles given in this brilliant book.

Simple in style and powerful in practice, the principles have been brought to life with personal anecdotes, superb examples, lovely metaphors and unbelievable insights.

While reading it, I felt as if I was sitting on a wonderful beach having a heart-to-heart conversation with the author as I basked in the warm glow of his amazing advice and got goosebumps after goosebumps."

P Venkatesh
TEDx Speaker, Leadership Coach

"Thrive is an exhilarating read. Going further than most books in that field, Lincoln's recipe is at the crossroads of motivational and business advisory content. Deeply rooted in the author personal's experiences, it is an honest and intimate look at his successes and failures from which he extracts lessons and advice useful to everyone, from employee to entrepreneurs. The chapters of the book are well organised, providing insights through the form of distinctions, and the reader will learn a lot in a fresh, dynamic text. With this book, truly everyone can Thrive."

Laurent Barrere

Lincoln Pan is one of the many influential people in my journey to becoming a now talented entrepreneur, Graduate in Business and a published author. Meeting him and following his methods of consulting were a big help in me understanding the commercial world of business and how you can individually stand out from the crowd. His book outlines a lot of the right things I've implemented in my journey to reach my current position specifically his diagram which explains the three versions of knowledge and or ignorance being "you know that you know", "you know that you don't know" or "you don't know that you don't know". Now if there's one thing I've learnt over time is that this principle is super valid. Exposure affects your inputs, outputs, feedback and environment and how you view the world, it forms the makeup and DNA of your mindset. Lincoln explains this flawlessly in his book "Thrive". A great read and if you are out there and anything like myself or Lincoln, hungry, driven, dedicated to change, leading the new business world and the pursuits of financial freedom. You'd be very wise to pick up a copy.

Sincerely,

Michael Assibey-Bonsu

Founder of Nectorclean.com
Author of 365 Days to Level Up purpose and Passion
Curtin University International Business Graduate

Lincoln Pan draws on his personal experiences to take you on a journey through his six THRIVE principles for practical success. This book is full of important information that puts you in control, helping you to achieve your goals in today's fast-paced, ever-changing world.

Conrad Pires, CEO, Picosat Systems

I have never found finance enjoyable or motivating, Thrive provided me with both! Lincoln has personalised this own finance journey, which helped me put it his knowledge into my own context. The information to garner from this book will set anyone up for financial success, whether they know their stuff or are just starting out. One of the best parts of the book for me was where to focus my energy. Beginning able to understand where I was currently at and where I wanted to be has been life-changing. I will be giving this book to my friends and family, it is a gift.

Nichola Zed,
Communications Lead, Contractor Engagement Solution,
Business Transformation, Finance
Rio Tinto Iron Ore

Acknowledgements

This book would not have been possible without the people and the teams around me—those people who have offered advice and words of encouragement, who have offered me space, and who have gently nudged me in the right direction. In writing this book, I have had the good fortune of receiving support from several individuals who have given me invaluable encouragement and advice. I am standing on the shoulders of giants, and I am outrageously blessed to have these people in my life. Thank you for being the powerful forces to shape who I am and what I am becoming. My deepest gratitude and love goes to all of you. I love you, thank you!

To my family: for your unconditional love and support.

I want to acknowledge my family—my parents and my two sisters, who stood by my side all the way, supporting and encouraging me through what has been a challenging and exciting journey.

To my parents, who dedicated the majority of their life to raising me in my early days and supporting me in my coming to Australia with their savings and who have always believed in me. For my dad (Yushu Pan), you have set the example of what great fathers and men ought to be: humble, loyal, and diligent. For my mum (Qiaoping Lin), thank you for the trust. Your kindness is always one thing I call home.

To my sister Xiaoyan Pan, for providing me with shelter and support when I had just arrived in Australia, including letting me use your garage as my first office when I had just started on my entrepreneur journey. To my sister Xiaohua Pan, for taking care of our parents while I am at Australia exploring opportunities. Thank you both for the trust in my entrepreneur journey. You are just like Mum—kind, generous, and caring.

To my mentors and coaches: for wisdom and guidance and for shaping who I am today.

For my wonderful mentor Tony Robbins. I started listening to your tape when I was a food delivery boy. Thank you for shaping who I am today and getting me inspired to become what is possible.

My other mentors are Ray Dalio, Jim Rohn, Eric Thomas, and Grant Cardone. Your books and seminars have all powerfully altered and shaped me into the person I am today. I am deeply grateful for your guidance and the paths you have set for me to follow.

To my close friends and business associates: for building meaningful work and meaningful relationships.

Chloe Zilli, Krish Vallipuram, Stephen Chipfunde, Samantha Campbell, Nichola Zed, Venkatesh P., Laurent Barrere, Piotr Siwek, and Sebastian Lang, thank you for being here for me. You all helped and taught me to believe in myself, keeping me grounded and focused while also giving me a laugh and a space to share when I needed one.

To my students and clients: for the opportunity to share my knowledge and serve you.

Thank you for choosing me—as a friend, as an adviser, as a teacher—to walk this journey together with you. I acknowledge you for taking on your life and creating abundant possibilities for yourself and your family. I acknowledge you for being a leader in the community, constantly creating value and making a difference. I acknowledge you for taking massive actions to thrive your financial future.

Finally, to all my friends, colleagues, students, and clients who may have felt neglected at any time during this writing project—the longest of my career—I hope you find that the final output justifies the absence. You've been in my mind and heart every day and every page.

Introduction

Who Is Lincoln? And Why Did He Write This Book?

> Give a man a fish and you feed him for a day. Teach
> a man to fish and you feed him for a lifetime.
>
> Chinese Proverb

As a child, one of my greatest fears was learning to ride a bike. I always tried to figure out how exactly the bike could move forward and still stay stable when it had just two wheels. In my mind, I always thought that I would somehow lose my balance and fall right off the bike. After two weeks of hesitation and procrastination, I finally took a leap of faith and got on a bike. I placed my left foot on the ground, positioned my right foot on the pedal, and gave it a push. To my surprise, however, the bike did not move.

'Look, this bicycle doesn't work,' I said to my mum.

My mum just looked at me and laughed, and then she said, 'Linc, you need to push, then put both feet on the pedal and pedal away. You are not stuck, you just need to move fast enough.'

Hesitantly and with extreme caution, I decided to give the bicycle one more attempt. This time, I pushed the bike with my foot that was on the ground, and immediately the bike started to move. I placed my leg back on the other pedal and started to pedal. The bicycle kept moving, and to my utter delight, I did not fall down. Till today, that instant where I overcame my fear of riding a bike is one of the most defining and exciting memories I have of my childhood.

I never understood how the bike managed to stay upright, and till today, I never learnt why. But what I do know is how to ride a bike.

I learnt two important lessons from my experience riding a bicycle.

1. The first lesson was that my mom was a great adviser. Whenever you face a challenge, mothers are a good place to look to for advice.
2. I am never stuck, and if I'm to stay upright and balanced, I just need to make sure I move fast enough.

I did not realise it at the time, but my experience learning to ride a bike would help me overcome all the uncertainty that was in store for me in the two decades after that.

I moved to Australia from China as a seventeen-year-old, and expectedly, it was a totally brand-new experience compared to what I was used to. At this period, I barely understood English, and unsurprisingly, it was one of the most difficult subjects I faced in school. I remember in school then, I was always that kid sitting in the corner, quietly doing his homework. I was very introverted and shy, so I barely talked to anyone. I had a heavy Chinese accent, so I found it quite difficult to communicate properly. As a result, I barely made any friends. *Depressed*, *anxious*, and *lacking self-esteem* were three of the most recurring words that came up any time my school counsellor described me. Seeing as I couldn't communicate properly or even make friends, I decided that maybe having a good grade in the university would help boost my self-confidence and also help me find a way to succeed in this new country.

Soon after graduating from the university within the top five percentile in academic performance in my school year, I was confident that my path to a good career was already rock solid. To my utmost surprise, however, I did not secure even a single job offer despite sending out 176 resumes to different companies and institutions. At this point, I had only $100 left in my savings account and eventually had no choice but to move back into my sister's house.

My sister had just had two newborn babies at this time, so I had to sleep in her garage. This period was the most depressing of my entire life. I was afraid of meeting up with my friends, to the extent of actively avoiding them, because I was afraid that they were all way ahead of me in the race to the top. I also couldn't call my parents, because I thought I had let them down.

'Why haven't you gone to get a job?' was the question my dad asked me most frequently in this period. Even over the phone, I could feel every bit of emotion in his voice. I understood where he was coming from. It was the wish and prayer of my parents for me to get good grades, acquire a college degree, and then get a secure and well-paying job. To help achieve this, they had spent a lot of time and resources on seeing me get through college.

On a day just like any other, I was seated in my ten-square-foot bedroom with a mostly blank mind. At this point, the future seemed so far away and bleak. I was reminiscing about my childhood, about that boy who was afraid of getting on and riding a bicycle and thought that he would never learn how to ride a bike. In that moment, there was a sudden flash in my mind as I remembered the little boy learning to ride a bike.

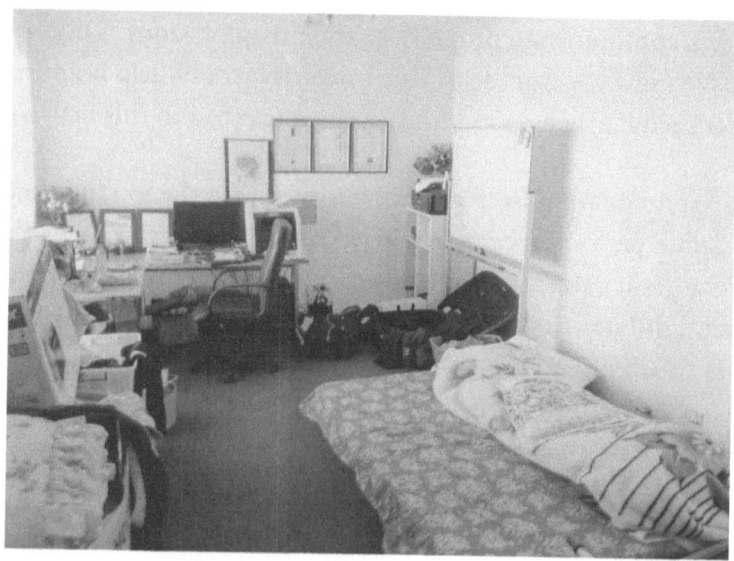

What if this situation I am presently in is similar to my experience of learning to ride a bike? What if I am not really stuck, and I instead just need to learn how I can move forward?

Instead of waiting on other people to give me jobs and offer me employment, why don't I work towards creating opportunities for myself instead?

Look, Lincoln, you don't have a job right now anyway, so even if whatever business you start does not work out, what is the worst that could happen? You fall back to where you already are now. So what exactly is the difference?

From that moment, my focus shifted entirely from passively waiting for someone to come around and offer me a job opportunity, to instead working proactively towards creating more opportunities for myself. From that day, I went to the local library and began reading several books on business, psychology, and personal development. I borrowed some training gear from a neighbour and began to train myself. Whenever I faced a setback or felt my motivation slipping away, I would think back to that little boy who was learning to ride a bike. 'You are not stuck. To stay balanced, you just need to move fast enough.'

Quite often, life shifts in a moment—the moment when we decide to lead our destiny, not follow a predetermined destiny.

Within the next few months, I got a night-fill job at a local supermarket. At night, I worked at the supermarket, and in the day, I read more than seven hundred books on several areas, including business, investment, and personal development.

It was not an easy journey. Soon after starting, so many of my business ideas failed that I even stopped keeping count. I made tons of mistakes, as I did not even know where to start or what to start with. Some of the businesses I started included weekend boot camps, an import-and-export business, teaching, accounting, and real estate. I even worked as a date organiser. I put every business idea I could think of into action. While many of them failed, some of them still exist today and are successes.

At this point, I should point out that the only thing that kept pushing me was the belief that I could offer something more than I already was. I believed that everything I was going through at that point was going to eventually serve a higher purpose.

Fast-forward to today. I am grateful to have had the privilege to serve and connect numerous clients across seven countries today. The period of darkness I experienced in the beginning has helped me lay the foundation of self-awareness and determination that I stand on today. Today here I stand, in front of 2,000 participants at this TEDx event to share my start-up journey. My businesses have given me the opportunity to reach thousands of people today, a feat I would have never dreamt of before. The joy of meeting with clients from seven countries and travelling to thirty-two countries over the past seven years has been phenomenal. The financial freedom every one of my businesses has given me has been more than I could have ever imagined. The joy of being able to connect and serve people across several borders has been immeasurable. In fact, I often feel grateful that I was unable to get what I thought was my dream job soon after I graduated from college, because if I had, I might be a depressed and annoyed accountant stuck at a cubicle, crunching and analysing numbers sixty hours every week for years.

Sometimes, not achieving your initial goal gives you the opportunity to discover your true destiny. Everything happening in your life happens *for* you, not *to* you. When we succeed, we tend to party and jubilate, but when we fail, we often ponder.
Whatever you are going through today will serve a higher purpose in your life; you just need to keep on moving forward.

Why Read *Thrive*?

> Success leaves clues.
>
> Tony Robbins

This book may have been written by me, but it is not about me. It is all about you. I dedicate this book as a reminder for you about how you can accomplish your goals and dreams by using some of the methods I used on my own journey. There are so many resources available for us today, but only if we are resourceful enough to realise and pay notice to the abundance which exists around us. This book is dedicated to waking you up to the fact that these abundances are in you and are you.

I set up *Thrive* as a reference book for future readers who aspire to thrive in any economic condition they may find themselves in, to give them a mind that is at peace to tackle whatever comes at them, and to guarantee that they and their family's future are secure.

Time has changed today, more than ever. Technology today has advanced the growth of businesses. Starting a business today is easier and at the same time more challenging than it has ever been. In this interesting time, the question is, how can we thrive in our businesses and our finance so we can have the freedom to enjoy what matters to us the most—our precious time with family and the people we love?

Even if you are not interested in starting your own business and would like to continue working with the company you're already employed with, you could still work as You Inc. In fact, I believe staying as a worker in someone else's company is more challenging than starting your own business, because you have only one client: your employer. Each day you go to work, you need to market your work to this one client actively, and if this client is unhappy or unsatisfied with your performance, you may be out of a job sooner than you can realise. In the very competitive market that we live in today, constant innovation and new ideas are always in demand if higher freedom is to be achieved. Technology today helps us start up businesses faster and easier than we could in the past, and this is both good and bad. People have often said these things to me: 'I hate my job, but I don't know what else I can do or where I should start.' 'I cannot afford to quit my job. I have over 100k in college loans to repay.' 'Running a business sucks. I don't know what my future will look like.' If you have also had these questions and thoughts running through your head, you should know that you are not the only one. Most people take step after step and live day by day, from pay cheque to pay cheque, without realising that there is a potentially better future ahead of them, just waiting to be discovered.

For fellow aspiring business owners, know that I am on your side. I have personally started and run more than ten companies over the past few decades; I understand the challenges you experience on a daily basis. I've also faced these questions: 'Where can I get more clients?' 'How can I get more money to pay for supplies?' 'What if the market crashes or melts down tomorrow?'

One of my close friends is a professional golfer, and he taught me how to play golf one sunny Sunday afternoon. I was quite eager to master the entire golf course within the five hours I was to spend there. However, the more I rushed to learn the process of the game, the more frustration I encountered on the way. My friend, noticing my frustration at the slow pace I was learning, smiled and told me, 'Linc, you have overcomplicated this game of golf. In golf, you just need to focus on the two-millimetre shift in your movement, and if you do this correctly, you are going to come out successful in the game.' If you hit the ball just two millimetres from the wrong angle, the ball will go in a totally different direction and can land up to two hundred metres away from the right direction. This same principle also applies to our life, doesn't it? If we can focus on changing our focus by even up to two millimetres, we'll find that our destiny will be altered in a very dramatic and surprising way. While we cannot arrive at our set destination overnight, we can work on changing our direction and trajectory overnight.

I dedicate this book to the future leaders who are willing to take up the responsibility for their financial life and act proactively to create whatever future they have envisioned in their minds. Being a leader is not just about having followers. It is also about living your life on your own terms. This book is about teaching you how to prepare yourself for the journey that is ahead of you and helping you develop an unshakeable mindset.

Having been in the business world over the past ten years and also having coached and consulted for hundreds of businesses and business owners across sixteen countries, I have seen a pattern emerge in businesses today. About 85 per cent of businesses disappear within three years of being created, and only about 5 per cent of businesses are able to survive past the ten-year mark. The bigger the business gets, the more likely it is for the business to fail. A great example of this concept is the story of the Lehman Brothers. I'm pointing this concept out to you, not so you get scared but so you know what the odds are, right from the onset. As business owners, we are less like chairmen in their offices and more like gladiators battling it out in the field for our freedom.

Almost every week, people approach me and tell me, 'Lincoln, I want to leave my current job and start my own business so I have more freedom to do some other things I want.'

My answer is often a stern no; having your own personal business does not mean you will have more freedom. If the major reason you have for starting a business is so you can have more freedom, you may end up spending more hours in a self-constructed prison.

However, starting and running your own business does give you freedom of choice. Running your own business gives you the freedom to decide who you are want to serve, the freedom to choose who you would like to work with, and the freedom to choose what type of legacy you want your business to continue with even when you're no longer in charge.

Welcome to the jungle!

When I first read of financial freedom as a concept, I thought it was just a dream. I thought it would never happen to me, that it was too far away a goal for me to attain. This was until the time when I started to plan towards it and work towards it, and now, fifteen years later, it is a part of my life. This financial freedom gives me the opportunity and the space to do the thing I am most passionate about: teaching.

Imagine you are at an amazing Italian restaurant. The steak is beautifully cooked, and the sauce drizzled on top is right on point. If you were to attempt cooking this steak yourself at home, you could either attempt a trial-and-error method for about five to seven years to be a master chef, or you could just go to that fancy Italian restaurant and ask the chef for the recipe, which would save you a lot of stress and effort in the kitchen. This is exactly why I have devoted hundreds of hours to writing this book: to be that chef that gives you the recipe book written from all my years of trial and error, learning, and experience so you can avoid having to experience all the stress I went through to learn how to cook good meals.

I have personally read a book per week over the last seven years. I have over five thousand books in my home library. While most of these books give me a taste of that delicious Italian steak, none of them have taught me how to cook one by myself. Most books on business focus more on strategy and tactics, while most books on psychology focus on human behaviour and emotional conditioning. My unique experience as both a financial adviser for businesses and a university teacher over the past decade has given me the opportunity and ability to see that these two areas can be extremely powerful, but only if a person knows how to combine them. Why is a business about people? Because businesses are started by normal, regular people like you and me to serve other people. By studying how we behave as business leaders, we can reignite our power towards serving our future clients better.

This is why I believe that this book can be your ultimate cookbook, giving you the ability to consciously and actively create and design your reality. If we do not actively design our own lives, someone else will hire us to build their own dreams. This is why this book has been written—to give you the road map to create the reality you have envisioned in your mind.

Now this cookbook is what we have called strategy in this book. The strategy is a specific and direct way to organise and plan your resources in order to produce a consistent outcome. It is like cooking a cheesecake. For this, you do not need to already possess thirty years' experience of cooking in a kitchen; you just need to know how to follow the recipe. If you can follow the recipe, you should arrive at the same results every time you cook.

See, you can start your business and try to attain financial freedom right now through trial and error, but it will definitely take you a couple of decades' worth of effort without knowing if it is the right way. However, if you can apply the principles stated in this book, you can save yourself the decades of trial and error. Do not get me wrong, I am not saying you will achieve your goals by following these principles without putting in effort or that you will get your results overnight. We all know that these types of claims to instant success are bull. What I am saying here is that by achieving these proven principles, you can achieve your goals more intelligently and more effectively than if you went ahead and winged it.

Knowing how to do something is not enough. Being able to actually do it is the key. How many times have you read something, maybe an article or a tutorial, that you know is very valuable, but you still did not take any action concerning it? Why does this happen? It is because intelligence and knowing are never enough, because knowledge is just potential power. True power aligns with the action. Only by taking action can knowledge be translated into practical and workable wisdom. I have attached each principle to the worksheet behind the chapter so you can have workable sheets and then take immediate action.

Over the past three years, I have interviewed over one hundred self-made millionaires. They have all come from diverse backgrounds, ranging from public company CEOs to small business owners and from scientists to engineers. This diversity put me on a journey to questioning what made these everyday people have unusual financial freedom, which most people desire but only a few people ever attain. By wealth, I mean that their assets could continue generating sufficient income to guarantee them the lifestyle they want. After having several conversations and developing close relationships with them, I began to understand that successful entrepreneurs are not really that different when placed side by side with other normal business owners. They have and feel the same emotions; they feel love, anger, hunger, and happiness. They face similar or even bigger constraints compared to small business owners. The only thing they do differently is in making decisions. Decisions determine direction, and direction determines destiny.

Think about the past few years of your life. All the decisions you have made in the past have contributed to you being the person you are today, haven't they? Decisions on who you marry, where you go to study, whether you start a business or not, etc. all shape you into who you are and who you will become. It is in the moment of making these decisions that your future is being shaped. My intention for this book is that it helps you make better and wiser decisions—those decisions that empower you and help you align with your true can-do nature and then make the impossible possible.

How is learning different from discovering?

There are three areas of our knowledge base:

1. You know you know (YKYK)
2. You know you don't know (YKYDK)
3. You don't know you don't know (YDKYDK).

YKYK refers to the things in your knowledge base you feel confident with: cooking, cleaning, writing, or reading.

YKYDK refers to the things in your knowledge base you know will be challenging when you undertake them, mostly because you do not know how to go about doing them. Examples of this include math, renovations, personal finance, and budgeting. You can often outsource these to other people who have these skills, or you can ask for help when you are stuck, because you are aware that you are challenged in these areas.

YDKYDK refers to things you are not aware that you do not know. This is usually where most failures stem from. We call it the blind spot. It is like driving a car and not checking your blind spot. The likelihood that this will result in an accident is very high. Let me share one of my experiences with a blind spot with you. Over the years, I always found speaking in public a serious challenge. Initially, I assumed I was an introvert, and since English was not my first language, I added that to my list of reasons. Soon after I established my business, I discovered that public speaking was an indispensable skill that I needed and couldn't do without, because I was going to have to make several presentations to my investors, as well as my employees. I recall one time when I needed to deliver a quick five-minute speech in front of a group of investors. As I stood up, my mind remained sitting. I lost every single word I wanted to say. The nerves I was experiencing from being told to give a speech without preparing overtook the ideas I had to share. After that experience, I took several courses in public speaking, such as Toastmasters. However, I still get a bit nervous every single time I have to talk in front of the public.

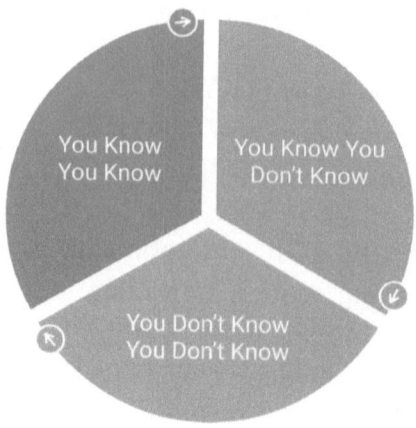

One time, by accident, I read a book titled *Feel the Fear and Do It Anyway* by Susan Jeffers. One part of the book really resonated with me. This part said that nervousness and excitement are the same emotional feeling, depending on the words we use to describe them. The words we use to describe the emotions we have often describe how these emotions make us feel and act. From then on, whenever I started to feel what seemed like nervousness when I had to speak in public, I would describe that feeling as excitement instead of nervousness. And it works! I no longer feel the nerves I used to feel when I have to speak in public. This year I did my TEDx talk in front of over three thousand participants, and I felt excited!

On the day that I had to give my first speech in public, I did not know that public speaking was my blind spot. It was that thing that I did not know that I did not know. Fortunately, by the time I had the TEDx talk, I had discovered my blind spot and had taken action towards overcoming the challenge it presented. This book is set up to assist you in finding and overcoming your blind spot so you can achieve your goals in a much shorter time than you previously thought was possible.

In traditional and formal education, teaching and learning are usually conducted between YKYK and YKYDK. For example, we have all been taught about gravity. It is a unique concept, and while you cannot see gravity, you can feel its effects. A physics teacher often relates an apple falling down from a tree as a visual and relatable example of how gravity works. This is usually how we are taught and how we learn new things: linking what we don't know (gravity and its effects) to what we already know (an apple falling from a tree). I have structured this book in this way to allow you to learn and discover between the known and the unknown. This is so you can maximise the time you will spend learning from this book and discover the possibilities that lie ahead of you.

This book is going to be a playbook that will equip you to thrive and flourish in any economic condition. We cannot control how the market will be tomorrow, but what we can control is the decisions we make, how we play the game, and how much we will give back.

If you have completed the six principles I have shared in this book and everything you have dreamt of has been surpassed, then I assure you that you will have everything you need to build a very successful business.

By the way, I can confidently tell you that the reason you think you are here, reading this book today, is not the real reason you are here. I can do this because I have consulted and taught more than three thousand business owners from over twenty countries in the past decade. In reading this book, you will derive the value you wanted when you chose to pick this book up, but you will also discover and learn more than you ever thought was possible to get from a book. This is what this book was written to do: teach you what you need and not just what you want.

Right now you are ready to learn from the next six chapters and the principles noted there. If you apply these principles and take action, you will end up having a breakthrough in your business. What will have changed in you by the last chapter? What will have transformed within you? You will not only get new strategies for business and finance, but you will also gain a new meaning to life.

The parts of life where you have been doing great will still continue to be great. However, the parts in which you have been lacking will improve too. Life will always throw challenges at you, whether in business, finance, or relationships. The secret is not to ask for less challenges but to become just as strong as your challenge is, and even stronger. You are more than anything that could ever happen to you, and you are bigger than every challenge or obstacle you may face.

How would it feel to know yourself at a higher level, not in a way that is problematic or dissociated but in one that is shown in how you run and organise your finance and your business? This higher self can help you break through your obstacles and limitations as soon as they show up.

What if, instead of being scared of the problem or challenge, you live for it? It is what leaders do. They solve problems and create solutions. What makes you a leader isn't the fact that you do not face problems or challenges. It is that you don't back down from a problem or challenge. Every problem you will ever face is an opportunity to grow. Are there any parts of your life that cause you pain and anxiety, such as your business, your relationship, your kids, your finances, or your health? You need to build up a part of yourself that you can step into and immediately have all your anxiety and fear disappear. The moment you step into this part of you, you can start to take action. The only way to keep fear away is to take action. Taking action helps move your focus from the matters that scare you and directs this focus to achieving the goals you have set.

What can the next six chapters teach you? It will not get you to be something you are not. It will help you uncover your real self so you have the liberty to run your business as it should be run.

I look forward to seeing the brand-new *you* at the end of Chapter 6!

CHAPTER ONE

Principle 1
Transform Your Mindset

It is not the strongest of the species that survives, or the most intelligent, but the one that is most adaptable to change.

Charles Darwin

Take a moment to look at the picture below. What is the difference between group A and group B?

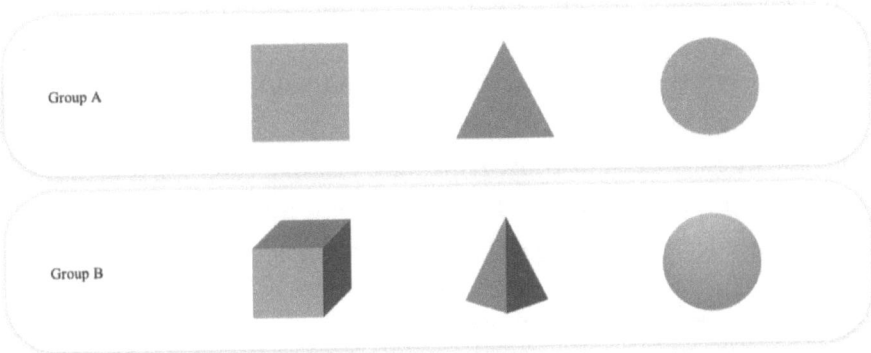

Yes, you are right. Group A is two-dimensional, while group B is three-dimensional.

Now what are the differences between two dimensions and three dimensions?

Three dimensions allow for greater scope and perspective, compared to two dimensions. Three dimensions allow us to see the perspectives that two dimensions do not let us see. Three dimensions are more functional when compared with two dimensions.

When we look at this, we can better understand how living three-dimensional lives is more holistic. Seeing in three dimensions allows us to lead with empathy. Not only is a three-dimensional mindset more enriching, but it allows us to act with civility, lead with empathy, and aspire greatly.

What if all these shapes represent different stages of your life? You only see one perspective until you transform.

In my case, while in college, I worked part-time in the fast-food industry as a restaurant manager. Like a square, I exhibited hard work, diligence, and perseverance, and I always strived for completion. I remember most of my night shifts ended at 1 a.m., after which I would head home to sleep and then wake up early enough to start getting ready for my 8 a.m. class.

I wanted everything to be under control and predictable. If I went on a trip, I wanted everything planned out exactly as it should be. I'm sure you can see how most of those trips were just like catching a bus in the morning—routine as usual. There was not a lot of excitement in my life, as I needed everything to happen as planned.

Challenge to be a square? Oh yes!

So I started my own accounting practice. In my mind, it was going to be a lot of fun, at least compared to the boring square life I was living before. I was like a triangle, driven and goal-orientated. Every week I worked sixty to seventy hours at the business. I sought to put in a lot of effort and be the best at all parts of the business. It was very difficult for me to admit the mistakes I saw myself making. I read one book per week to improve my knowledge. Everything I did was all about my work and achieving my goals. Needless to say, I had no close friends, as they could all sense that I was all about my goals and not much else.

After a while, however, I was still not happy about who I was, so I decided to change. As such, I began to study the philosophy of Buddhism: 'What goes around comes around'.

I took six months off work to travel, see the world, and experience different cultures. I became interested in interpersonal relations and focused on building good relationships, as well as on my health and well-being. Whenever the business was not going well, I told myself, 'It is just the energy circulating. Things will get better.' I became very interested in other people and their worlds. I realised that I felt their pain and joy. At this point, I thought I was already the most spiritually awake person I could be.

After a while, however, I still did not feel happy at all. Every time I changed, I always stuck to that new shape for a while until I ended up feeling empty again. Still, I didn't know how I could possibly change any more, as I had changed three times already. What else could I change? What if I felt disappointed again?

Have you ever changed but still felt empty after a while?

After deep reflection, I realised that throughout this entire time, I had been focusing on the change, but I had not been transformed. I had changed from job to job, duty to duty, function to function, but the problem was that I remained two-dimensional. When I faced challenges in my life and business, the common approach I took was to do more, do it faster, or in other words, continue with business as usual. I could keep changing my role and job functions forever, but the root causes of the challenges I faced were always going to keep reappearing.

What are the root causes of this challenge?

I focused on *changing* instead of *transforming*.

A transformed person can see the limitations that a changed person cannot see. A transformed mindset can take in different views of the dimensions and appreciate the limitations of the different pathways. Furthermore, a transformed mindset can see the overall big picture. Here are some examples.

Square Transformed into Cube

A math teacher teaching algebra.

A math teacher with a changed mindset thinks like this: 'I teach algebra. Algebra combines numbers and letters, and all my students need to learn this in order to pass the exam.'

A math teacher with a transformed mindset thinks this way instead: 'I am a math teacher, I teach algebra to future engineers, accountants, and artists. I am going to do my best to share this part of knowledge so my students can use this knowledge to whatever extent they want to.'

Triangle Transformed into Prism

A business person facing growth challenge.

A business owner with a changed mindset reasons: 'I am going to spend more money on advertising so I can reach more people. I am going to offer more products and services to the customers I have already. I am also going to reduce the price of our service.'

A business owner with a transformed mindset instead thinks: 'This business represents who I am, so if I'm weak in an area, the business could be weak in that area too. It is not just about what I should do, it is more about who I should be in order to achieve the goals I desire. If my business is not growing, am I practicing the growth mindset? What are my objectives in this area? I am going to focus on where I want to go, not on what I am afraid of.'

Circle Transforms into Sphere

A yoga teacher facing personal finance challenges.

A yoga teacher with a changed mindset thinks: 'I really enjoy what I am doing, but working on my passion just does not pay the bills. I need to figure out another career pathway or take on a side job to supplement my income.'

A yoga teacher with a transformed mindset thinks: 'I understand that I feel a bit upset about my personal finances right now. I enjoy the lifestyle I have created for myself and the contributions I can make towards other people around me. Instead of seeing personal finance as a challenge, there is a lesson I need to learn from here. Have I been resourceful? How can I create more value for my existing clients? Have I considered the possibility of transforming this yoga class into a business venture? What is my vision for my personal finance?'

Once you have transformed, you can still be the driven triangle and retain your original identity, but now you can expand to see more perspectives if needed. It is like a folding chair; if you need a chair to sit on, you can just pull the chair out and stand it as a functional portable chair. From square to cube, from triangle to prism, from circle to sphere, it is a state change.

What is the difference between change and transformation?

Change is external, while transformation is internal. The external environment is always changing: economy, politics, culture, market conditions, etc. However, what is important is not the change that happens in the external environment but how we perceive this change—our internal dialogue.

So let's look closely at the areas of business and personal finance. How can we transform our mindset in the matter of a couple of distinctions?

Quite often, when we think about our financial life and business, we usually say, 'If I have a sufficient amount of money, I will do the things required to achieve my financial goals.' It is like when we try to lose some weight; we think about finding the perfect diet plan and a good personal trainer, and then we do whatever we think is necessary to achieve the weight goals we desire.

If these thinking principles are correct, why do 75 per cent of weight-loss participants regain their weight after twelve months of their program? Why do 10 million Mega lottery winners become bankrupt after five years?

Why do only 1.5 per cent of businesses ever survive past the ten-year period?

It is because they direct their focus to what they have to *do* instead of what they need to *be*.

I suggest reverse-engineering the sequence into this:

What I suggest is reverse engineer the sequence into:

Be that person who possesses the necessary qualities first, then you will find that it is much easier to do the things that are necessary to achieve your set goals and get the things you desire.

For example, when talking about relationships, if you want to start a relationship with the partner of your dreams, you need to be the kind of person you would want to date first. Be compassionate, be a listener, be understanding, and be caring. Then you will do the things that attract this kind of person to your life. Take consistent action to fulfil his/her needs: send her flowers, call her in the middle of the day to say 'I love you' for no reason, go hiking in the mountains. Once you build a loving character, you will take the actions that are natural. It is about who you are, not just what you do.

Finally, you are going to retain your dream partner for the long term, not just for a short-term arrangement.

To be successful in business, you need to hold the business mindset first: be goal-orientated, driven, determined, and resilient. After you have successfully done this, you will then be able to take the steps that are necessary to achieve your goals, such as reading books, attending seminars, seeking feedback from mentors, and taking consistent action, irrespective of what the results are. The moment all this has been done, you can then proceed towards financial freedom.

> It is not because you acquired million-dollar assets; it is because you have become a million-dollar person.

Businesses come and go, but being the type of person who can build and sustain a successful business—the type of person who is resourceful and can attract resources—is what this chapter on transformation seeks to show you.

There are three distinctions to transforming your mindset in business.

Distinction #1
Four Sources of Income, Not All Paths Are Created Equal

The process of starting a business is in itself a process of transformation. Let's take a step back to see where we normally earn our income from. After being a financial adviser for about eight years, I had reviewed over ten thousand individual and business financial statements. I came to realise that there was a pattern to our sources of income and started to appreciate the different advantages and disadvantages of those sources of income. The diagram below represents the four sources of income that the majority receive:

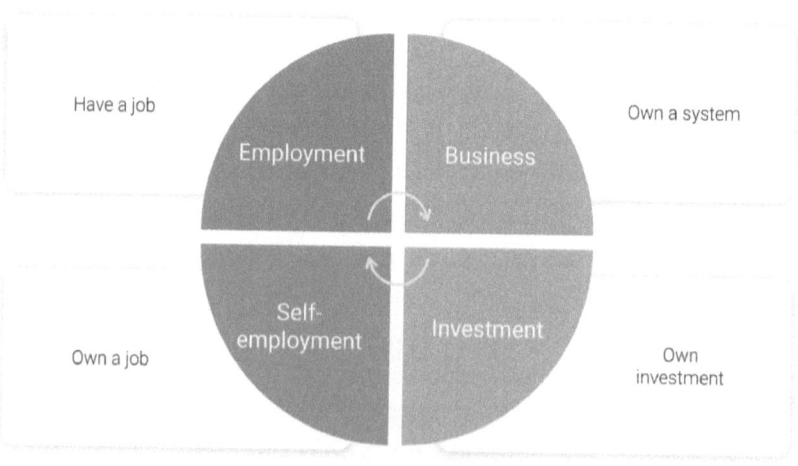

Resources: Cash Flow quadrant by Robert T. Kiyosaki

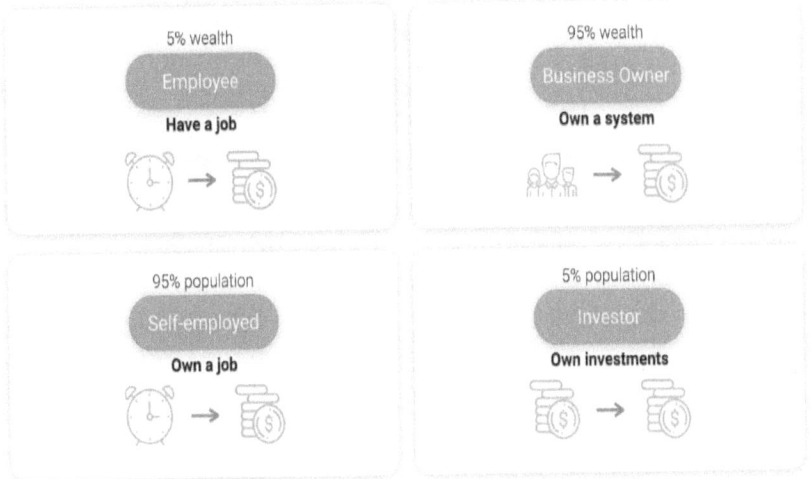

Source: *Cashflow Quadrant* by Robert T. Kiyosaki.

Those four main sources of income are:

1. Employment
2. Self-employment
3. Business/Corporation
4. Investment

A. You Can Earn Income in All Four Paradigms

A lot of us in the world today have the potential to make a living from all four income paradigms. Which paradigm you choose to earn your primary income from is not dependent only on the skills and information we learnt in school. It's more reliant on the person we are at the core. What are our strengths, values, weaknesses, and interests? These core differences are the factors that attract or repel us from the different paradigms. All four types of employment can earn you a living and even make you a fortune. It is like choosing a transportation method—taking a bus, car, bike, or airplane—to go to work. All those forms of transportation can take you from A to B, but it really depends on your personal preference.

However, irrespective of the kind of work we do, it is still possible to earn income from all four sources. If you were a dentist, for example, you could decide to make a living by getting employed as a member of staff at a large hospital or in an insurance company. You could also choose to work in a government health institution.

Another option for a dentist would be to toe the self-employment line and establish their own private practice, rent office space, hire staff, and have their own set of clients.

A dentist could also choose to be a business owner and start up a dental practice franchise and then have other dentists as part of his staff. To assist with the logistics of the business, this dentist could employ a business manager to handle the administrative aspects of the business. In this case, the dentist is the business owner, but he does not have to be in charge of the day-to-day running. If the dentist so chooses, he could start up a business that does not involve anything about dentistry and continue to practise dentistry as an employee at another business. If he does this, he will be earning dual incomes, both as a business owner and as an employee.

A dentist could also become an investor in other people's businesses or in institutions like the stock market, bond market, and real estate, and generate some more income.

Whichever decision he makes, the important thing to note is 'generate income from'. What matters most isn't what we do exactly, but how we generate income. It is about where we get the money instead of what we do to make money.

B. Different Income Paradigms Require Different Beliefs and Strengths

Above all, the variations in the features that shape us—our interests, values, likes, dislikes, strengths, and weaknesses—are what push us towards the different quadrants we choose to make our money from. Some people love working as an employee under other people, while some others hate it. Some people are okay starting and owning a business but are not willing to run them. Some others love owning the business and being involved in its day-to-day running. Some people are happy to be investors, while some others cannot get over the fear and risk of potentially losing their hard-earned money. A lot of us have some of these traits inside us. To be successful in any of the four income quadrants, we have to redirect some of our core values.

A great example is a client of mine who is a very successful freelance artist. She was considering establishing a painting school that she would then, after a while, turn into a franchise. Suddenly, she became overwhelmed; she no longer felt the passion for painting. Instead, she now saw painting as a transaction between her customers, her students, and her time. However, the moment she goes back to her inner core—being a freelance artist—she will be able to return to her previous self and enjoy painting again.

Which paradigm of income are you comfortable with?

The main characteristics of these four income paradigms are summarised below:

	Advantage	Disadvantage	Key psychological drive (KPD)	Key language
Employment	—Secure income	—Tax —Growth of income	—Certainty —Security	—I want a safe, secure job that offers good pay and other great benefits.

Self-employment	—Security of employment	—Growth of income —Time constraint	—Certainty —Security	—My hourly rate is $150. —I have more than thirty hours to devote to this project.
Business and corporation	—Tax —Freedom of choice	—Cash flow —Initial set-up —Growth	—Freedom —Growth	—Why do the work yourself when you can employ someone else to do it, and maybe even do it better?
Investment	—Tax —Freedom of choice	—Cash flow —Unexpected risk	—Freedom —Growth	—What are the risks? What are the rewards? —Does my return on investment justify the amount of risk I am taking?

C. You Can Be Rich or Poor in All Four Income Paradigms

Having been a financial adviser for the past ten years, I have seen people making high seven-figure salaries on all four types of income. I have seen some of my clients go bankrupt even with all four income types. It is really dependent on the person, not so much on where they get the income. You have to understand that it is very possible to be rich or poor in each of the four income paradigms. In each of these income paradigms, different people become millionaires, while others end up becoming bankrupt. Earning in one paradigm or another does not automatically mean you will achieve financial success there.

D. Not All Paradigms Are Equal

By identifying the different characteristics of the various paradigms, you'll be able to make more informed decisions on what paradigms may work for you and which ones to avoid. For example, one crucial factor that led me to opt for the business and investment paradigms is that they offer tax advantages. Legal tax breaks are also available in the employment and self-employment paradigm, but those in the business and investment paradigms are much more sustainable. In the business and investment paradigms, I could earn money faster and make use of this money for other projects longer without having to give up a lot of it to the government as taxes and fees. I believe everyone needs to pay taxes, but no one is obligated to pay extra on taxes.

Another incentive for me to work in business is that I have the freedom to control what type of business I work on and what type of business environment I work in. If the business structure was not to my taste, I could change it. Compare it with employment, wherein you usually can't alter what the job description requires you to perform, as it is part of a legal contract. Additionally, in a business, you can have as many clients as you want. If you lose one client, it will usually not have a major impact on your income. However, if your income is from employment alone, you only have one client—your boss. If you happen to be redundant and get laid off, you will have lost all your income.

Love what you do, but have multiple streams of income.

E. Paradigm Shifts Require Different Ways of Being

When people ask me, 'Why don't you get a job?' my reply is usually 'What for?'

Our schools have conditioned us to be good students and then graduate to find well-paying jobs. This system was designed very well back in the 1900s, during the Industrial Revolution period, as more employees meant more productivity for the factories, which then resulted in more tax revenue for the government.

However, things have changed since then. Yes, we do still need accountants, lawyers, dentists, engineers, teachers, etc., but there are so many other ways to generate income. Realising the fact that employment is merely just one form of income will liberate you and unleash your creativity.

Uber, Airbnb, digital marketing, and Blockchain—there are so many new ventures and opportunities waiting to liberate us from trading time for money.

This is the era of awakening and creation.

While money is important to me, I did not want to spend most of my life working solely to earn. This was why I did not seek to only have a job. I wanted to be a responsible citizen, but I also wanted to have my money work for me instead of having to strive for it most of my life.

It is my strong belief that there is so much more to life than just working to earn money all day every day.

That is why understanding that having different types of income streams is important. It depicts the different ways money is generated. There are several ways to be responsible and make money while not having to always work physically towards it.

F. Different Income Paradigm, Different Cash Flow Stream

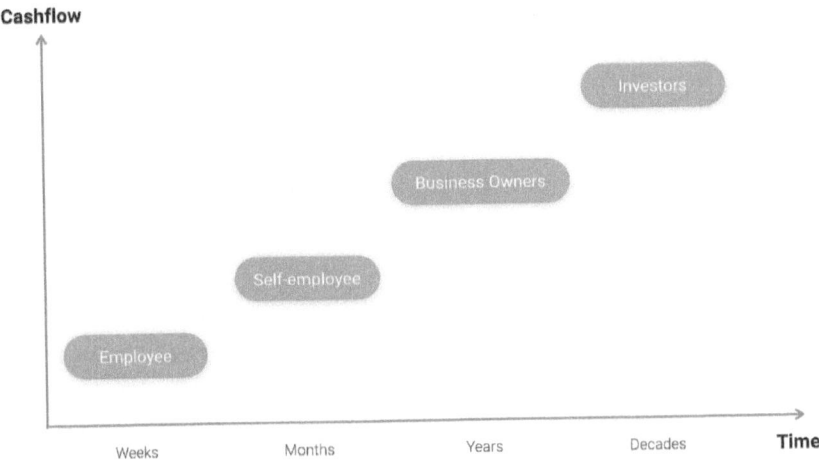

Different levels of income streams require different capacities in terms of cash flow duration.

For employees, depending on the employment, you would expect to get paid weekly or monthly.

For self-employed individuals, you would need to take into consideration the suppliers and customers. Sometimes it can take months for your invoices to get paid. You also need to factor in the bad debt and credit cards; the cash flow is slower than employment in some ways.

For business owners, it can sometimes take years to generate your first profit, as a significant portion of whatever you earn needs to be reinvested into the business.

For investors, you will get paid for three to five years or an even longer period. An often-quoted saying goes, 'Employees are overpaid at the beginning but underpaid over the lifetime. Business owners are underpaid at the beginning but overpaid in the lifetime.' Why? On your first day as an employee, you know very little about the company and how it operates at best, yet you still get a salary; after three years in the company, you have almost mastered everything on the job, but you still get paid a similar range. On the other hand, in starting a business, you need to do all aspects of the business: marketing, selling, business development. If you don't generate visible and measurable results, no client will be willing to pay you. It is the most underpaid 'job' you will have in your lifetime. But once the business gets established and starts to run properly, you start to receive the dividends of getting income 24/7. This is the very reason people choose business as one of the most effective vehicles to wealth.

You see, different levels of income streams require us to have different perspectives on cash flow expectations. Most people hesitate to start a business because they are concerned that they will not get paid, like when they were employees. Understanding the difference between the types of cash flow will allow you to liberate your expectations as you set out on a new venture.

G. It Is More Than the Paradigm

These four different income sources are more than just where we generate our income from; they are also about how we choose to live. Digging deep below the mere surface of this diagram, you will see completely different worlds and different perspectives on how the world runs. Personally, I have viewed the world from different sides, so I can state outright that the world looks different on both sides.

However, this does not make one quadrant better than the other. Each aspect has parts that make them great and parts that can be problematic. This book aims to give you insight into life on the different quadrants and show you what parts of you need developing if you are going to be successful in them. I believe that it will help you gain better insight into the life path that you should be on.

A lot of the skills that are necessary for success on the right side of the quadrant aren't taught in school, and this shows why people like Steve Jobs, Bill Gates, and Mark Zuckerberg did not finish college but still learnt how to be successful at business and investment. This book will point out the features you need to possess if you are to be successful in the business and investment quadrants.

First, I will give a brief preview of the four quadrants, and afterwards, I will proceed to in-depth analysis of the business side and all it entails.

By the time you are through with this book, you may decide to make a change in your income, or you may decide that your present income source and state works just fine for you. You may even decide to branch out into one other income paradigm or two more, or just decide to partake in all four paradigms. As humans, we all have our differences, and one paradigm is not more important than the other. In society, people need to participate in all four paradigms to ensure that the society retains financial stability.

The older we get and the more experience we gain, the more our interests change and evolve. Looking at today's world for example, a lot of young graduates are at first okay getting a job at a company. After a few years, however, some of them decide that the corporate path and all its hierarchical issues are not for them. This change in mindset develops as they get older and gain more experience, and it causes them to look for other sources or opportunities to grow, be challenged, earn money, and find happiness. I hope that by reading this book, you discover some fresh ideas to help you achieve these goals.

To summarise, this book is about helping you find a place—a home in a paradigm or in several paradigms, where you can earn and be happy.

Distinction #2
You Get Paid for the Value You Create, Not Your Time

We all have twenty-four hours, seven days a week. We sleep for eight hours, work for eight hours, and spend the other eight hours with family and friends. What exactly separates our income?

You may say it is hourly wages. Yes, I agree that hourly wages are a factor, but it is not all the factors. Think about what determines our hourly wages.

When I worked as a delivery boy at Domino's, I got paid $11 an hour; now when I run a seminar, I earn $10,000 in a couple of hours of teaching. The average public company executives earn over ten times the average company employee. Why is that?

It is because people do not get paid for their time; instead, they get paid for the benefits and value they provide the market with their time. The key word here is *market*. You could be a valuable member of the community. You could be an invaluable believer in the church. But your pay scale is directly related to the marketplace.

When I was a delivery boy, I got paid for delivering the food from A to B at the agreed time. Because I did not add much value to the product, I only got paid for the time I spent delivering. When I perform as a financial adviser, I help my client reduce their tax bill by at least 20 per cent or boost their investment returns by another 25 per cent. This is the reason they pay high fees. It is not because they enjoy travelling thirty minutes to drink coffee with me; it is because I provide them with a lot of value in the time it takes to drink a cup of coffee.

We do not get paid for our time, but we get paid for the value and benefit we create in the time we spend. The more value we can create in the time, the more we will get paid. It is like when you go to see your dentist; you don't care how much time he has to spend to fix your problem, as long as it is fixed. *You pay for his solution to your problem, not his time.*

By understanding this point, you see what I really mean when I say business is the single fastest way to create value and get the income you deserve.

As a company employee, you usually get paid a predetermined rate. It is nearly impossible for your boss to give you a pay raise that is ten times higher in the next twelve months; my old friend still works at Domino's Pizza, and his pay has barely adjusted with inflation over the years. But in the business world, you can get paid exponentially higher amounts of money. If you can create enough value in the marketplace, money will follow you everywhere. Think about Uber, Airbnb, Apple, Amazon, etc.; how these companies are part of our daily lives now; and how tremendous the value they create is, as millions of people's lives have been impacted by their products and service.

My motto for financial freedom is 'Impact millions, earn millions'. Everything you want to have can be yours; you just have to help enough people get what they want.

Business is the place to exchange value and generate income; investment is the platform to generate cash flow.

Most people believe investment is the place to earn a fortune; that is why they invest in index funds and retirement plans. But the underlying assumption and condition is, you need to wait another thirty or fifty years to get your 2 million in retirement money, and only if the market is still functioning as well as planned. What if the economy is not stable? You have no control whatsoever. That is the very reason the top 10 per cent of wealthy people use real estate and shares to generate investment cash flow to maintain their lifestyle. Thinking about it now, if you have

1 million in savings, your investments on average generate a 10 per cent return; now you can have a 100k passive income to fund your lifestyle. The challenge here, however, is that you need to already have a large asset base of up to 1 million. This is why I emphasise value creation, not value in the future. Business and the marketplace are where we can exchange value and earn our asset base so we can invest our money away to get the lifestyle we envision.

Let's recap our discoveries so far:

1. We don't get paid for our time; instead, we get paid for the value we bring to the marketplace with our time.
2. The more value we can create, the more monetary reward we are likely to get.
3. Business is a very effective vehicle for exchanging value, and investment is the best place to generate the required cash flow to fund our lifestyle.

Distinction #3
Transformed from Consumer to Producer, Business is One of the Fastest Vehicles to Create Value and Increase Your Income

Business is about translating your ideas from invisible to visible. It is about creating more value than your competitors do and doing it well enough for your customers that no other business in the market can compare with the value you offer them. The word *business* derives from the Old English *busyness*. My understanding is, if you are busy serving others, your problems will disappear. My mentor Jim Rohn used to tell me, 'You can have everything you want, if you can just help enough other people to get what they want.' Business is the channel we can use to help other people get what they want.

Starting a business is a quick way to translate your value into the marketplace and live life as you want to. It is the most profound way, but it is not the easiest way. Most of us have been programmed into nine-to-five work routines. We went to school to get an academic education. The school trained us to be professional accountants, lawyers, engineers, and doctors. There is nothing wrong with those occupations, and our society needs these professionals to function effectively. However, the wrong thinking is in believing that these professional degrees are the only way to achieve financial freedom. In fact, I believe your job and profession are totally different from your financial blueprint.

Our schools and societies have conditioned us to be *consumers* instead of *producers*. But all the cash is poured into the producer side, not the consumer side. That is the reason 67 per cent of the population are not ready for retirement after age sixty-five; they have been on the consumer side of the equation for too long.

Imagine what you can do if you can:

- become a publisher and publish books instead of only reading books
- offer classes instead of just taking them
- lend money to people instead of just borrowing
- hire people in need of jobs instead of looking for employment yourself
- hold a mortgage instead of taking one.

Break free from consumption, switch ideas, and reorient your world as a producer.

How to enter the world as a producer? Start a business.

Why is business the better choice compared with employment, property investment, and share investment?

These are three good reasons:

1) You have complete control over the products and service you are offering, and most businesses can be started with less than $1,000. You can't achieve that with property investment. For the investment to bring the desired return, you need to set aside three to five years for the investment returns. However, there is one factor you cannot control, and that is time. No one can tell you when the property market will go up or down. Same as shares on the market. You have no control over how the share price is going to perform as a minor shareholder of a company.
2) You do not have to first work for ten to twenty years. Business can provide you with the cash flow to invest in shares and the property market. In other words, a business can give you a more flexible income stream to fund the lifestyle you desire.
3) As an employee, your biggest constraint is that you only have one client; meanwhile, if you run a business, you could have as many clients as you want. There are no limits on the amount of profit you can earn.

Here are some ways to earn a million dollars:

- Salary $50k × twenty years
- Salary $100k × ten years
- Salary $250k × four years
- Earn $114 per hour, every hour of the year
- 5,000 people buy a $200 product
- 2,000 people buy a $500 product
- 10,000 people buy a $100 product
- 1,000 people buy a $1,000 product
- 5,000 people pay $17 per month for twelve months
- 2,000 people pay $42 per month for twelve months
- 1,000 people pay $83 per month for twelve months

- 500 people pay $167 per month for twelve months
- 300 people pay $278 per month for twelve months.

Pumped? We are just getting started. Next chapter, I am going to share with you what it takes to transform your business idea from zero to hero.

CHAPTER TWO

Principle 2
Hustle Your Way Up

Without hustle, your talent can only get you so far.

Gary Vaynerchuk

In Far East China, there is a special kind of tree called the Chinese bamboo tree. Unlike most trees in the world, the Chinese bamboo tree takes up to seven years to grow. In this time, it has access to everything a tree requires to grow—fertile soil, water, nutrients, sunlight, etc. In the first five years, there is barely any physical sign that a tree has been planted there. By the fifth year, however, a shoot appears. Immediately after this shoot appears, the Chinese bamboo tree grows up to thirty metres tall within seven weeks.

Now the question is, did the Chinese bamboo tree really grow thirty metres tall within five weeks, or did it do so within five years? The answer is quite obvious. It grew thirty metres in five years. This is because, if it had been denied access to the necessary factors that it needed to grow any time within that first five years, the tree would have died there in the ground.

In this same way, I can see people approaching the guy watering and fertilising the ground even though there was nothing to show for it yet.

'Hey, what are you doing? You've been out here a long time, man.'

'Word around the neighbourhood is that you're growing a Chinese bamboo tree. Is that right?'

'Yeah, that's true.'

'Well, even my three-year-old son can see that this tree is not growing. How long have you been working on your dream, yet you have nothing to show for it? Is this all you have to show for it, just some empty soil?'

People will often do that to you.

Some people stop trying because they don't see the results they want instantly. They stop because it doesn't happen quickly.

Do you aim to see your visions and dreams become your reality? You have to continue to water your dreams regularly.

All this may not happen as fast as you would like. Several events will happen on the way that will find you off guard and unprepared. As such, you have to deal with these issues as soon as they appear. You also need faith and patience to drive you into action.

You have to keep moving and keep plugging away.

In these hard times, you may not know how you're even going to pay your employees. In these times, you may fail, and things may not work out. However, one thing I have discovered is that while you work on your dream and vision, the harder the challenges you face, the sweeter the victory afterwards is.

Why is this? This happens because in spite of all these challenges and struggles, what you evolve into in the process of achieving your vision and dream is often more important than what the dream itself was.

The person you evolve into is often more important than what you have achieved. The character you build. The courage that you start to manifest. The faith that you develop.

One day, you will wake up in the morning and stare at your reflection in a mirror and find that you are now a different person, that you now have a different kind of spirit inside you. People can then see you and understand that you know what life is. They see that you have now embraced life.

The journey was hard and difficult, but you went through it anyway. If you don't try anything, nothing is possible. If you try, at least you have the hope of getting it done.

In a basketball match, there are two different groups of people: the audience and the players on the court. These two groups of people hold different mentalities.

The audience is sitting in their seats, watching, complaining, cheering, and chatting about how the game should be played.

The players are on the court, playing the game. They are out there on the pitch making things happen.

Now this is also how the game is in the game of life. The question now is, are you going to be the audience, or will you be a player in the court? Are you just going to talk about it, or will you start to make it happen?

I have to admit it, I get afraid sometimes too. For a long time, I have put off writing this book you are currently reading. Every time I saw a bestseller on Amazon, I would get inspired to be one of them, to share my ideas with thousands of readers and possibly help millions of people achieve financial freedom, like my mentors Tony Robbins and Robert Kiyosaki are currently doing.

However, there is always a voice in my head saying, *Lincoln, who do you think you are? Stop wasting your time. Look, you barely passed high school English. English is not your first language, and you can't even write well enough in your first language, so what makes you think you can write a book in a foreign language? No one is even going to be interested in your stories, and besides, your ideas are not unique, so why bother spending hundreds of hours writing a book no one is going to read? Stop making a fool of yourself.* When I shared my book idea with my dad, he said, 'It is a great idea, Lincoln, but I feel it is a very challenging thing to do. Who is going to buy and read the book?' I put off the idea of writing this book for the past three years. In all my business successes, this little voice has always dominated my actions towards the idea of writing a book. Every time I did a public speaking seminar, I've had people ask me if I have written any book, and I have always smiled and said, 'Yes, it is coming.'

While we are busy chasing our dreams, we often take advice from the people that love us and let their voices influence us. Because we love them, we try to avoid hurting their feelings, as we would rather keep our inner feelings and opinions hidden. Sooner or later, when we wake up one day, we see that there is only a limited number of things we can do about our future. This is not because we can't; it is because we don't. We think about what is appropriate, and this need for appropriateness keeps us locked and constrained in a box. We find ourselves stuck. The question is, what will you do? Are you going to quit chasing your dreams, and will you go back to that small box and let everyone else except you be happy?

One day, when I travelled to Florence, Italy, there was a beautiful lady playing the piano at midnight on the street. She played one of the best music pieces I had heard in my life. However, there was no one around or on the street to listen to the song. I stood there for about half an hour until the music stopped. I then walked up and asked her, 'This is great. Why don't you choose a better time to play, like in the daytime? There would be more people in the street then, and you can get more attention and money then.'

She just smiled and gave me a reply I would never forget throughout the rest of my life. She said, 'I played the music because I am a musician. I don't play for attention and money. This is who I am, and it is what I am committed to doing. I do not mind if it is midnight or right in the middle of the day. For me, *now* is the perfect time. Yesterday is history, today is a mystery, and now is *all* I have.'

At that point, I gave the lady all the coins I had left in my pocket and headed to my hotel to start Chapter 1 of this book.

Our *now* is all we really have, isn't it?

Every time I begin to doubt myself as I write this book, that conversation is what pumps me up and pushes me to keep going. There is enough criticism available out there, so why don't I give myself a chance to make my dreams become a reality? If I tried, I had a fifty-fifty chance of either succeeding or failing. If I hadn't tried, however, I wouldn't have had the chance to share my ideas and stories with the world. The biggest challenge I face is me. Why should I even care about what other people think about me? I should be more concerned with how I think about myself and my commitments. It is not what people think of me that matters, but it is what I think of myself that shapes who I am destined to be.

In order to influence other people, I have to first be influenced. In order to lead, I have to first be led.

If I was not excited about a book I was writing, how would I expect my future readers to be excited? If I saw this book as a waste of time, why would my future readers think differently about it?

By writing this book, I have said *yes* to myself. I am my first reader, and I am my first fan. I have to have 100 per cent belief in the value that this book brings to the table.

Once I changed my mindset and my outlook, I was more determined than ever to write this book.

Just to let you know, even without this book being launched yet, there are already over three hundred pre-orders on the mail list.

This chapter is more than just a couple of motivational strategies designed to pump you up for the journey ahead. I am going to share two distinctive points to not only help you grow your business but also help you grow yourself.

The Need to Focus on Your One Thing

A person who chases two rabbits at the same time will catch neither.

Confucius

In February of every year, I fly back to China for the Chinese New Year. The Chinese New Year is a very important festival in Chinese tradition. All family members get together to celebrate their reunion and harmony. The part that makes me happy the most is not only getting to see my mum but also getting to taste her cooking, as it brings back a lot of my childhood memories. At New Year's Eve, my mum cooks over twenty dishes, which are put on the round dining table. One of my weaknesses is that I can't avoid trying to eat every dish on the table. My stomach often ends up full; I can't walk around, so I just lie on the sofa for the rest of the evening.

After learning this lesson the painful way, I rearranged my diet plan. I became very selective and would ask myself, 'Lincoln, if you could choose 20 per cent of the food on this table, which ones would you choose?' Then I choose these dishes. My stomach usually feels much better afterwards, and I actually enjoy the food instead of thinking I need to finish them all. (My mum usually thinks I'm overthinking it. 'Just finish your meal, son,' she says.)

Why do I feel much different? It is because I chose to eat consciously. I chose to eat intentionally. I chose to eat purposely. This distinction is what changed everything else.

The Chinese have an old saying: 'A person who chases two rabbits will catch neither'.

The rabbit conundrum is an illustration of the results of failing to decide. The word *decide* has the same Latin root as *scissors* and *incision*—to cut. In this case, you are cutting off the debate and selecting one of the options you have available to you and cutting off the other options.

Here you commit your focus and actions to the path you have decided on and chosen. If you are not certain, if you have not yet committed, if your decision is not firm, you face the rabbit dilemma. What will you do when an option opens up? You would have another decision in front of you, losing time and possibly both opportunities in the process.

This is not saying that you cannot change your mind or make different decisions. However, you should make a strong case that what you are currently doing is not in your best interests and that you should be pursuing a different rabbit. When you do decide on a rabbit, stay focused on that rabbit, or you will forever be chasing and never catching. That does not sound like fun to me.

Stop reading for a moment and think about the things that bother you so much in this moment, the things you think you need to do urgently.

When you think about this to-do list, do you feel lighter or heavier? Is it empowering you or dragging you down? Keep that feeling and the to-do list in your head while you go on to read the rest of this book. We are about to discover how you can be liberated from this to-do list and get laser-focused on what really matters. When I adopted this exact concept to my business, the business had a revenue boost of over 200 per cent in about six months, and I had more free time for the things that I wanted to do the most, such as writing this book.

Ten years ago, I had just started on this business journey. I tried to do everything well, and I tried to do everything by myself. I tried to multitask also: doing marketing on Facebook while I was on the phone with potential clients; preparing presentations for investors while I was looking for properties to buy; coaching my business associates while thinking of replying to urgent emails from my clients.

As you can imagine, it did not go well. I ended up getting overwhelmed by the amount of workload ahead of me. I was totally flat out. The business also did not get any better, and the quality of my work started to get depleted, causing my clients to question my ability to deliver the results they wanted. Eventually, my initial passion for work began to reduce day after day.

This was until one day when I decided to commit to one thing, and one thing only, until it had been done fully.

The issue is not that there is too much time for us to do what we want; it is that we often try to fit too many things into the limited time we have.

Discover how you can prioritise in order to protect the resources you have, such as your willpower and time. Don't let thinking small limit how large your life can be. Think bigger than you are now, aim higher than you think, and be bolder than you already are.

See how big you become in life.

How do you stay on track of everything you need to do? Most of us probably already have a to-do list. If you already have one, you need to know that everything on your list does not have equal priority. Some items have a higher priority than the others. But can you identify which one is a priority and which one isn't?

The best answer is to apply the Pareto principle to your advantage. Pareto's studies indicated that about 20 per cent of people living in Italy owned about 80 per cent of the land. Other people deduced that this principle may also apply to other areas of life, such as 80 per cent of the results we see being the product of 20 per cent of our efforts.

Apply this Pareto principle to the list you already have, and you can decide on the issues that are most important to you and the life you want.

What is that thing I can do that would make every other thing easy or unnecessary?

We see the people who are on top as stern and disciplined. Studies have shown that everyone has limited resources, and one of these limited resources is discipline. The best way to go about this is to apply the amount of control that you have to creating new habits. A lot of people think that success or failure is a result of single actions that make you a hero or a zero. This is actually not the case. Success or failure comes from your daily habits, which you have accumulated over time. If you are overweight today, it is not a result of the last fast-food meal you ate. It is the accumulation of all the unhealthy eating over the years that results in you having a weight problem. This same thing applies to having an amazing and healthy body. If you have a healthy body, it is not because of that one time you went to a gym. It is because of all the consistent exercising and dieting day in and day out. Our habits are what make the difference.

What is the fastest way to form a habit? By allocating your limited willpower to a few selected number of tasks.

We often see our willpower as a constant, never-ending resource. Yet our willpower is more accurately comparable to a vehicle's fuel tank. As we go about the activities of our day, we use up significant amounts of our willpower. To cite an example, if you have to concentrate fully on a lot of tasks in the course of the day, you may find your willpower dropping lower and lower.

Remember the Chinese New Year example I gave earlier? Our attention is like our stomach; it has a limited capacity. So use your limited attention wisely. Use it intentionally. Not everything matters equally; choose where to focus your attention.

This is why you should make your most pressing and important decisions early in the morning, when you still have a lot of willpower. One of my business mentors from McKinsey & Company said, 'Lincoln, imagine you eat a frog every morning. If you do the most challenging tasks in the morning, your day is going to get better and better. However, if you do the less challenging tasks in the morning, you will end up having to solve your most important tasks at your least resourceful time, and this will not give you the best possible results.'

With discipline, you can develop new habits, like taking a walk regularly or knitting. The moment this new habit becomes one with you, you'll be able to add another one. Habits do not consume willpower, because they're second nature already, which is why they're important. What is that thing that could positively benefit your life if you did it frequently?

When you try to work and juggle several tasks at once, you often have to move between tasks. The moment you have to change what your attention is on, you lose valuable time, because having to switch back to the task has a time penalty attached. For example, if you try to juggle marketing and accounting simultaneously, your brain needs to work on two totally different tasks at the same time. When you start and stop between the tasks, your brain will get exhausted between the tasks. It is like your iPhone running too many apps at the same time; it will reduce the CPU speed. Your brain would only function at 50 per cent capacity at the task you value. This is why so much of our time is wasted: we think we can give the best of ourselves by doing multiple things at one time.

A business owner loses about a third of their daily work time because of distractions and having to refocus. They try to do all the tasks at once without setting priorities. Replying to emails and making phone calls are urgent but not necessarily important. Even when the urgent is good, the good can keep you from the best and from making your unique contribution, if you let it.

When I operated my financial advisory business, I employed a proactive and intelligent business analyst. Once, after he had worked with me for a few months, I asked him to work on some pressing issue that I needed addressed as soon as possible. He said, 'Lincoln, I will do whatever you want me to do. Just let me tell you about my situation.'

Then he showed me his activities planner, where he had laid out the whole project timeline, together with performance criteria. The deadline had been carefully negotiated before. He was a very effective and efficient worker, which was why I had come to meet him initially. I believe that if you want something done, have a busy man do it.

Then he said, 'Lincoln, to do the jobs that you want done right would take several days. Which of these projects do you want me to delay or cancel so I can do what you need?'

I didn't want to be responsible for that. I didn't want to slow down one of my most productive workers because I had a crisis I was handling at the moment. The job I wanted was pressing, but it was not important enough to disrupt his schedule. So instead I found someone else to do what I needed.

We say yes and no to things daily, usually many times a day. As I work with different groups, I tell them that the essence of effective time and life management is to organise and execute around balanced priorities. Then I ask them, if you were to place yourself in one of three areas, which would it be?

1. the inability to prioritise
2. the inability or lack of desire to organise around those priorities
3. the lack of discipline to execute the tasks around them and to stay with your priorities.

The challenge here is not managing time; it is managing ourselves.

What about all the incoming networking invitations and new potential business opportunities? Remember that time your friends called on you over and over to check out a new 'life-changing opportunity'? If you wanted to remain focused on just your own business and didn't want to make your friends disappointed, what should you do? It is pretty simple: just say no.

Want to have more free time and more focus on the things that actually matter? Learn to say *no*.

At the 1997 Worldwide Developers Conference, Steve Jobs said, 'You would think focus means saying yes, but it actually means to say no.'

When Steve Jobs returned to Apple, he cut the product line from 350 to 10. He said no 340 times. That's a whole lot of nos. But look at Apple's market valuation of over 1 trillion today; you'll see that he was right.

I remember my biggest challenge when I started out in the business. It was telling too many people yes too many times; I often had to overstress myself to actually deliver on the promise on time. When people asked me to look at their new business ideas, another additional stream of income and a new potential partnership to join, I couldn't resist but say yes.

When I learnt how to say no, I thought it was rude in the beginning. But then my thinking has changed. *No* means 'I am not interested'. It is nothing personal. It protects your time and that of the people who invite you. It reduces the opportunity cost for both sides. It actually creates sustainable value for both sides by providing a clear and direct response.

> Experience is knowing when you should say yes;
> wisdom is knowing when you should say no.

A journey of 1,000 miles starts with one step. Take one step after the other, and soon you'll notice that you have travelled really far.

Business and Financial Success Are Forged by Process, Not by Events

All successful businesses work by a carefully curated process. They have and use all the processes and recipes. Regardless of what you may be aware of, successful businesses do not just happen; they are not events. Successful businesses don't appear out of the blue or come from a movie show. It doesn't knock on the door, standing on the porch with balloons and a large check. Financial success does not just exist out of nothing.

Most people overestimate what they can achieve in one year, but they underestimate what they can achieve in a decade. If I could go back in time and tell twenty-year-old me something as I was starting out in business, it would be that I should be patient. I often find myself rapidly evaluating situations the moment I face them, which can be either a blessing or a curse, depending on where it leads. When it turns out well, this ability to assess issues quickly helps me quickly understand a situation and create a way forward.

When it turns out bad, however, this thought process creates a space between me and co-workers and employees. I often find myself jumping to conclusions while others are still trying to understand the information. This 'ready, aim, fire' syndrome occurs a lot with entrepreneurs, and while it may promote rapid growth and expansion, it can often result in more issues that are problematic.

In my experience, the conclusions I arrive at are not as strong as I assume they are. Sometimes I ignore important details and opportunities, and I don't think the implications through. Other times I become impatient and end up excluding the people I am supposed to be working with from the plans I make. Anything that's actually worth it takes some time. It does not just happen in a day, whether it is a skill or a new business idea.

Although entrepreneurs like me like to make matters work as simply as possible, the fact of the matter is that the world itself is a complex place, full of layers and nuance.

What if building a successful business and achieving financial freedom are like cooking a moreish dinner for your family? How would you approach this game differently?

Business and financial success are a process, not an event. Walk up to a chef today, and they will tell you that the perfect dish is made up of a combination of ingredients and a perfected process. Add a little bit of this, some more of that, and do all these with the right amount, at the right time and at the right place, and that's it! You have just cooked a tasty meal. The preparation of the meal, execution of the dishes, and delivery of the dishes is the process; having a delightful meal is the event. Wealth creation also follows a similar process before wealth is generated—a combination of many different features and ingredients to form something valuable and worth millions.

Wealth eludes most people because they are preoccupied with events while disregarding process. Without process, there is no event. Take a moment and reread that. Millionaires are the results of following a working process, and the events you see and hear are what emerge in the course of that process. For our chef, the *cooking* is the process, while the *meal* is the event. For weight loss, regular exercise and a healthy diet are the process, while the weight loss is the event.

For example, an athlete who scores a 100-million-dollar contract to play pro basketball is an event from a process. You see and hear about the big contract, the spectacular get-rich event, but you typically ignore the process that preceded it. The process was the long arduous road you didn't witness. The daily four-hour practices, the midnight pickup basketball games, the torn ligaments, the surgery and rehabilitation, being cut from the junior varsity team, and the resistance to the neighbourhood gangs—all frame the journey that forms the process.

When a twenty-year-old sells his Internet company for $50 million, you read about it on a tech blog. The event is lauded and showcased for all to admire. An Airbnb start-up is the process. You don't hear about the long hours of coding the founder had to endure. You don't hear about the cold, dark days of working in the garage. You don't hear about how the company was founded on credit cards at 21.99% interest. You don't hear that the company founder slept on friends' couches while building the business. You don't hear about the founder and his rusty POS Toyota with 300,000 kilometres.

When Colonel Sanders founded Kentucky Fried Chicken (KFC) in 1952 and opened over twenty thousand stores in 123 countries in less than ten years, the accomplishment made headlines around the world. What doesn't? The subtle facts of the process. Like the fact that Colonel Sanders started his business at age forty. That he almost went broke one year after founding the company. That to carry the business forward, he blew through $30,000 in his personal savings and later $60,000 in credit card debt. The billion-dollar get-rich outcome is the event; the process is the struggle and the backstory.

The valuation of my businesses surpassing 10 million dollars is an event, but its progress was carved by the process. Outsiders see the nice house and the expensive cars and might think, *Wow, if only I could be so lucky*. What they do not see is the process I went through: the failure of starting up three previous companies, almost going bankrupt twice, and the daily rejection. Such a belief is a mirage of event over process. Wherever wealth is created or exists, it is often preceded by hard work, trial and error, risk, and countless sacrifices. If you seek to jump past the process and arrive at the result, you'll never experience life-changing events. Unfortunately, the media-driven get-it-now-not-later society we live in today celebrates the event itself but ignores the important process that brought about the event. If you look deep enough, however, you will spot the process buried under other descriptions of the event. We are in a society now where emphasis is on the results; the means barely get published. We are overwhelmed by the information, but we are starving for wisdom. We go to school to get an education; the intention is to get a job. Well, if you think it through, it is something more than that. The jobs you get are the by-products of being educated through school. The process is the means to the end. Going to school to get educated is the process; getting the job is the end.

When you finally make your first million, it will come as a result of the process you went through, not because of some imaginary twist of fate or a lucky break that just happened to you. Process is what leads to wealth and success, and while the destination may often be the most visible and celebrated, process is what shows you the way.

Imagine if you had to explain to a potential buyer how every part of your business works and integrates with other parts. Now think of yourself looking on as your employees describe to the potential buyer what they do and how they do it. Imagine how elated and impressed this buyer would be in the face of such order and control.

Most people only pay attention to the final product of successful entrepreneurs. They say, 'I could never be like them. They just got lucky.'

But most don't see what they have overcome: all the struggles, the daily rejections, the hardship, the criticism, the empty bank accounts, and all those lonely nights trying to make their vision become reality.

You only see that the differences between the one who quits and the one who doesn't are:

- they show up every day
- they work hard every day
- they hustle every day
- they learn from a group of mentors every day
- they improve every day
- they do all these things even though they feel like quitting every day.

Eventually, they become who they are today. Yes, the elevator to success is out of order. You will need to climb the stairs.

CHAPTER THREE

Principle 3
Recognise Your Strength

Everybody is a genius. But if you judge a fish by its ability to climb a tree, it will live its whole life believing that it is stupid.

Albert Einstein

A beggar had been sitting at a roadside for about thirty years. One day, a stranger walked past, and a conversation ensued. 'Have some change for me?' pleaded the beggar, pulling out his old begging bowl.

'I have nothing to give you,' said the stranger. Then he asked, 'What's that you are sitting on?'

'Nothing,' replied the beggar. 'Just an old box I have been sitting on for as long as I can remember.'

'Ever look inside?' asked the stranger.

'No,' said the beggar. 'What for? There's nothing I need there.'

'Have a look inside,' insisted the stranger.

Eventually, the beggar opened up the box, and surprisingly, the whole box was filled with gold.

Today I am a stranger without gold to give you but who is encouraging you to look inside yourself—not in a box like in that story, but inside yourself.

'But I am not a beggar,' you may say.

People who have not discovered the true wealth which lies inside them, which is that radiant joy of being and the unshakeable confidence of being who they are, are almost the same as beggars, regardless of how much material wealth they have. They are looking outwards to find fulfilment, validation, security, pleasure, and love even though they have all these and much more inside them already.

In this chapter, we are going to take a step further to explore who we are and what our natural strengths are, so we can align our future career and business with the nature of our talents. The four distinctions I share with you in this chapter can help you uncover how you see yourself and, most importantly, how to build a leadership team around you so you can all progress towards achieving business goals effectively.

Distinction #1
Pain + Reflection = Progress

Back during my MBA study days, one of the most valuable experiences I had was that of starting an import and export company (Red Swan International Inc.) with my wonderful study cohorts. There were three co-founders in my team, and we had vastly different backgrounds: a financial adviser, an artist, and a professional corporate manager. It was a very challenging journey at the beginning because we all had strong beliefs and ideas about what should be the priority of the business. We tried to identify what was the most important aspect of business so we could devote most of our time to figuring out that part first. It is like a domino; the first piece needs to be placed in the right direction so the other dominoes would follow on the right course. For me, as a financial adviser, every business strategy in my head tends to be viewed from a financial technical aspect. The questions I ask myself are often like this: How do we get the funding, and where can we invest the initial profit so the business can be self-sustaining? How can our investment achieve a higher return of investment (ROI)?

My other team members' points of view were quite different from mine.

Melissa, the artist, had questions like 'How can we create the best products in the market? I want our products to become the new identity of imported Chinese goods—high quality and slick design.'

Lisa, the professional corporate manager, had her questions more along the line of 'How do we structure the company? We should have clearly defined roles and functions in the departments, and allocated duties for each personal.'

Of all three of us, who was right? What should have been our business priority?

The answer? We were all correct. We all communicated from our own strengths and our unique professional backgrounds. We all wanted the business to be established the way we wanted it to be—just like how we operate ourselves. If you have a kid, look at them; most of the time, your kids are like a mini version of who you are. As you raise your kids the way you believe is best for them to be raised, the same thing applies to your business. We had a mental blueprint of how things should be set up. There was no right or wrong answer here.

The key points of distinction here are:

1. Understanding the differences in our mental framework. Realising that we all think differently. There is no correct way of thinking, but there is an efficient way of listening which is critical for business success. When you run a business, listening is as important as speaking, as listening allows you to assess your team and clients' mental framework so they feel like you understand them. When they feel understood, they are more open, and you are able to influence them instead of just getting excited and forcing your ideas on others.
2. The businesses we build represent who we are. Whatever our strength aligns with, the business is going to show up with this strength. So we need to think objectively: What are my strengths? In which areas do I shine the most? How can I utilise my strengths to help other people shine?
3. By understanding your strengths, you can build your team more effectively to complement the areas you have a weakness in. In other words, if you are strong in marketing but not so good at accounting, you can build the entire business based on your strength in marketing, and you can hire or outsource the accounting and financial aspects to an accountant. This allows you to focus on the things you are good at. Remember, no one pays you for the things you are not good at; people only pay you for the things you have absolute competitive advantage at in the marketplace. If you want to make every area your strength, you will end up with nothing as your strength.

Back to the MBA story. As soon as our team realised our various strengths, we went back to listening to the input of the various members. We discovered that our strength is in our diversity in culture and professional background. Instead of placing priority on each area, we shared the common vision and built on each other's strengths. We no longer thought of our different points of view as being the top priority; instead, we contributed and subsidised each other with different perspectives. When the artist, Melissa, wanted to design the best products available in the market, I showed her our current financials, and we worked out a realistic product budget. Lisa, on her part, worked on structuring the logistics to make the products ready for the market.

This business was very successful, and it was featured in the graduate school business case study.

Sometimes we tend to be negligent about what we are good at, and we instead spend all our focus and energy on improving the things about us that are not so developed. If Albert Einstein had been placed in a team to play basketball and he failed the game, should he feel humiliated? Should he feel like he had underperformed? I don't think so. Look, he was the top genius in the world of what he did. If you evaluate yourself based on the things you are not good at, you will always feel like you are not enough.

Understanding our weaknesses is important so we can build a team to empower our mission and appreciate our strength, so we can contribute to others.

No one is good at *everything*; you just need to choose one area where you are naturally gifted and focus on building it up.

> You can literally have anything you want, but you can't have everything you want. Be like a postage stamp; stick to one thing till you get there.

Distinction #2
Artist + Operator + Manager = Well-Designed Business

Where do businesses come from?

A lot of businesses today are founded by individuals who are deeply passionate about their 'new ideas' (the artist/entrepreneur) or who have a special skill, such as an accountant, engineer, plumber, or electrician (the operator/technician).

In the world of business success, three primary roles must be performed: artist (creator), operator (technician), and manager. It is like trying to design a Lamborghini supercar; every piece has to be placed at the right position, so when the time comes for the car to hit the racetrack, it can accelerate from 0 to 100 kilometres in 0.2 seconds with ease. If you put a giant V10 engine in the small frame of a Hyundai Excel, the V10 engine will tear the car into pieces. The power from the V10 engine will override the structure of the Hyundai Excel. In the words of architecture, form flows function.

In other words, the artist (the car engine), operator (the car wheels), and the manager (the car frame) are all equally essential in creating a successful business (the supercar).

To build a business, three unique skill sets are necessary:

1. the entrepreneur—supplies the vision
2. the manager—supplies order and system
3. the technician—produces the output.

Although each of these three personalities want to be the boss, none of them are interested in being a boss. Still, each of these three skill sets are needed for success in business.

The artist converts a little matter or situation into a huge commercial opportunity.

Artists (creators) are dreamers that have their eyes set on what the future should be. They have visions about the possibility of the future. An artist is like a car engine—powerful. An artist is highly creative. Artists love their ideas and their art. They live to create art and find producing it highly energising. Most artists would love to commercialise their work product and have millions of customers applauding its creativity and beauty, but they make the faulty assumption that the key to more applause and higher sales is tweaking the product. In other words, if they could only improve their art, they could make more money. If McDonald's were run by an artist, the management team would spend the majority of their time trying to create a healthier and better-tasting burger. Clearly, the artist in McDonald's has retired decades ago. On the other hand, Steve Jobs was a full artist during his first ten years with Apple, and it almost destroyed the company. After twelve years, when he returned to the company, he equipped his artistic nature with some business acumen (managers), which allowed him to successfully create one of the greatest businesses of the century.

Managers are pragmatic.

Managers maintain order and institute systems and processes where they're needed. Basically, managers focus on what happened in the past, and they fashion the entrepreneur's dreams and visions into a practical and well-structured framework. Managers are like a car frame. They protect the engine and provide the framework of the operation. A manager focuses on creating a structure or machine that relies on various moving parts doing their job synchronistically to achieve a common outcome. A great manager runs the business end of the business by measuring results and then either fertilises the activities that produced the good results or changes the activities that resulted in the bad ones.

Technicians like doing things.

Technicians exist and work in the present. They are hands-on people who like to do the work that needs to be done, and they like to do so without getting interrupted. Technicians are the wheels of the car. They make the vision and structure become reality by running mile after mile, day after day. Operators focus on getting things done. The erroneous belief is that the harder they work, the more they will make. Most operators spend so much time racing around and putting out fires that they never get the chance to figure out who is starting them. New ideas and opportunities are difficult to take advantage of because there simply is no time to notice these ideas and opportunities. The operator is not running the business; the business is running her.

Relating this to my own business journey, I started up my own business as a tax accountant. Instead of being employed by the Big Four accounting firms, I believed I would be better off starting my own accounting business. The first three years were a real struggle, as I was still in the technician's mode of operating. Every week, I spent over sixty hours in the business, but I did not spend enough time *on* the business. The marketing, public relations, and human resource aspects of the business were being totally left out. If I hadn't realised that I was a business owner and not a business operator, I would still have my head stuck in endless paperwork in the office.

A typical business-builder personality is:

- 10 per cent entrepreneur
- 20 per cent manager
- 70 per cent technician.

A very good business builder would be:

- 33 per cent entrepreneur
- 33 per cent manager
- 33 per cent technician.

	Artist (Creator)	Operator (Technician)	Manager
Focus	Passion	Time + effort	Leverage + measure
Plan	Create it (Fun)	Control it (Sweat)	Structure it (Machine)
Strategy	Start it ('I love my idea')	Do it (React)	Lead it (Coach)
Outcome	Fulfilment (Hobby)	Business runs you	You run the business
Motto	'If it is not fun, I am not doing it.'	'If it's going to get done, then I will have to do it.'	'Measure results. Change activities.'

Distinction #3
Business Mastery ≠ Artist Mastery ≠ Technical Skills Mastery

A lot of businesses that are created today are created by technicians—people who have skills and enjoy doing what they are doing and decide that they would prefer to work on their own than have to work for another person. The idea of an entrepreneur who created a business purely out of the goodness of their heart is a myth. Most times, businesses are created by people who are skilled in something new and technical, and who decide to become entrepreneurs and start their own business, as opposed to letting someone else reap the profits for their own work.

At the beginning, when the business is smaller and lacks resources, the founder must fill all these roles, which is why small business owners are often tired and stressed. Over time, as the business gains mass and traction, additional personnel can be added to the team to leverage the performance of any or all these roles.

While passion and technical competence are extremely important, they are of primary value in the 'getting traction' and 'creating a niche' stages of growth. After a certain amount of time, size, and momentum, more passion and enhanced professional skills are not the primary drivers of growth and sustainable business success.

Artistic success requires refinement of creative and artistic talent. Operational competence requires honing professional and technical skills. *Business success requires mastery of business skills and tools.*

It is like cooking different dishes; different ingredients and cooking methods are needed to produce the tasty dishes. If you use the same procedures to cook the different dishes, you will end up with frustration and disappointment. *Insanity is doing the same thing over and over again and expecting different results.*

As a business grows (gets traction and scales up), the additional skills required to evaluate and seize new opportunities, create enterprise value, and sustain momentum are all business related—managing cash flow, hiring the talent, reading financial statements, creating a culture, refining the target market, designing the messaging, leveraging other people, etc.

I, as a business owner for example, didn't start out as a business owner. It was not my focus. I started as an accountant. I had the technical background (the operator), and I really enjoyed helping clients achieve their full financial potential and get more confident with their personal finance. I actually perceived myself as an artist, with every client I had part of my creation. I wanted to create financial success for all the clients I had the opportunity to share my knowledge with.

I had a giant vision—to help everyone achieve financial freedom so they could have the liberty to work whenever they want, with whoever they want, and wherever they want.

With my vision, sitting at the office and meeting only a couple of clients a day was just not scale enough to fulfil my goals. So I started my coaching and teaching business, with the intention to reach out to more people. After a while, my technical strength as an accountant (operator) and the desire to help clients liberate their financial success (artist) became less and less effective in the business. The business turnover had hit its plateau. Also, I was exhausted every day from working on the field. This was the reason that made me ponder and wonder what the missing ingredient to making my business successful was.

A lot of business owners, especially new ones, assume that just because they understand how their product works, they also understand how the technical aspect of the business would work. However, these two aspects of business are distinct and require different skills, and ignoring the differences between both can be disastrous for business. When talking about new businesses, being able to do the needed technical work is more often a liability than it is an asset. Why is this so?

1. Business growth skills have a higher priority and importance than just generating output at the initial stage.
2. The technician may find that the job they love eventually becomes stressful, and they have to juggle a lot of stuff that doesn't excite them as much as the reason they entered business in the first place. Eventually, they enjoy the technical aspect of the business less.
3. After a while, the business builder comes to realise that the technical aspects of the business can be easily contracted out to someone else. The real value that the business creates is dependent on the business-building tasks, which may not interest the technician and is more hard work.

To explain the above points using an example: One of my clients, John, has worked as a chef in a fine dining restaurant for the past thirty years. One of his dreams is to open a fine dining restaurant franchise of his own across Australia and serve food to people who love Italian fine dining. He is a great chef with an extreme passion for food and people. However, I told him his skills could be a liability that would prevent his business from going to the next level. Why? Let's break down the business-building process using the three points above:

1. Business-building skills are far more important than the mere production of output for any new business. To build his new fine dining restaurant franchise, his ability to understand the marketing, business operation, human resources, accounting, and legal perspectives of the business is more important than knowing how to cook. McDonald's is one of the most popular and successful franchises in the world today, yet the kitchens boast of no master chefs and the food is cooked with anything but. However, the business keeps on growing year after year. This is because the business is system reliant, as opposed to being people reliant. If McDonald's needs to open an additional 100 restaurants, they don't need to hire 100 new chefs, because the business is scalable. This is what is meant by business-building skills being more important than the production skills. Of course, the business owner being able to maintain the high standard of food is a plus, but the great business skills still have to be on ground too.
2. The technician realises that he no longer enjoys the work, as he has to juggle multiple other tasks, making the work less fulfilling than it was at the start. To start his new fine dining franchise, John needs to know how to manage all areas of business: accounting, marketing, finance, human resources, and legal. All these areas are not as appealing in the same way as John's passion for cooking. On most days, he would rather stay in the kitchen to cook, as opposed to preparing PowerPoint slides to pitch to potential investors. This is what sets apart

a chef from a business owner. John needs to know a little of everything in the business. This doesn't mean he needs to do everything by himself. As a business owner, he needs to know how to delegate these vital tasks to the professionals so he can have more time to do the things he enjoys the most—cooking.

3. After a while, the business builder comes to realise that the technical aspects of the business can be easily contracted out to someone else. John realises that in becoming a business owner, he needs to work *on* the business instead of working *in* the business. He can contract all the cooking tasks out to others by hiring a chef or creating recipe books for the business. These tasks are essential aspects to becoming a business owner.

If all these bases are not covered, new business builders may find themselves becoming disillusioned and discouraged with the progress their business is making.

Distinction #4
Three Business Development Stages

Infancy, Expansion, and Maturity

Building a business is like raising a child. If you can anticipate the different stages of the child's development, you have the ability to handle whatever challenges will come at you. Because you can predict the challenges and set up the business structure for different stages of business needs, you will be able to progress through the different stages of the business with ease.

Take a moment to think about the different stages of human development—from infancy to adolescence, from adolescence to mature adulthood. From the perspective of Maslow's hierarchy of needs (diagram below), we have different psychological needs in the different stages of our human development. Therefore, different forms of mentorship need to be set in place to help us reach our full potential.

Sources: Maslow's Hierarchy of Needs

Infancy. Our parents take care of us day in and day out. We need to stay with our parents, as they provide us with a feeling of safety and protection.

Adolescence. Our schoolteachers and workplace managers are needed to make sure we learn and are trained with a sufficient amount of knowledge and skills. At this stage, we start to feel the need for freedom and growth.

Mature adulthood. After we're done with school and have gotten some years of working experience, we are now able to understand what path we should be headed in and what career path we should pursue. You start to understand that the person you are becoming is a higher priority and is more important than whatever you do daily. At this stage, we feel the psychological needs of connection and contribution.

Once we understand the different stages of needs, we can then develop a strategy to meet these psychological needs in the business. We can continue building the business with a clear sense of direction, detailing where we are going and how we plan to get there. Like a growing child, each stage of business development has different priorities. Like a parent raising a kid, each stage of building the business requires that the business owner looks at the business needs objectively.

Most businesses move through three stages of growth:

1. infancy—when the technician is at the fore of the business
2. expansion—when management skills are in high demand
3. maturity—when an entrepreneurial outlook to the business is necessary.

A lot of problems often arise when a business is operated based on the owner's wants instead of what the business requires. In truth, businesses have different needs at different stages of their development.

We should always run two businesses at the same time: the business we are in now and the business it is going to turn into in future.

The business we are in now is going to give us the cash flow, and the business we are going to turn into is going to give us the opportunity to thrive.

Stage 1—Infancy

At the infancy stage, the technician is the entire business. Take away the technician, and the business ceases to exist. Infancy ends the moment the technician decides to make changes so the business can grow and move forward. If these changes are not made, the business will eventually crash and burn. If made, however, the business can then proceed to the adolescence or expansion stage.

If you are a talented writer and you just started a creative writing business, at the infancy stage, you are the business. If you stop doing the writing work, the business ceases to exist. When a kid is at the infancy stage, a lot of attention is required from the parents. This is also the same way in business. When the business is in infancy, you need to devote a sustainable amount of your attention to building the business. Marketing, paying invoices, finance, and delivering the work are all handled by you. Until you are willing to concede that there is a better way to run the business and take action to build the necessary framework, the business will stay as it is forever.

Stage 2—Expansion

At the expansion stage, things may begin to go well, and more and more clients may start to sign up for your business. There is a momentum evident in the progress of your business. You start to build teams around you and delegate the tasks that need to be carried out to some extent. However, you may still find yourself looking at a glass ceiling, in the sense that you have limited time available to handle all the demands you receive from your clients.

Every business owner has their own comfort zone—a set of tasks and responsibilities they feel comfortable delivering on:

- For a technician, it is how much work he or she is capable of.
- For a manager, it is the number of employees or people they can coordinate or manage.
- For an entrepreneur, it is the number of people who buy into their dream and vision.

As soon as a business expands beyond this zone, the business owner can take four possible actions in response:

1. Get small again—This means scaling the business back to the infancy stage, when the owner had a higher degree of control on the company. (This is usually the first inclination for most technicians-turned-owners.)
2. Go for broke—Attempt to expand the business fast enough so it generates enough money so the business owner can hire the resources the business needs to manage itself.
3. Hang in there—This is done with the hope that if the business owner keeps going, he'll finally get a break and succeed eventually.
4. Push the business to maturity—For this, the business owner has decided to open up and learn new skills and also set some new priorities so his limited time can be used well.

Stage 3—Maturity

A business attains maturity when it develops a realistic sense of its journey to its current position, as well as an accurate understanding of what it has to do to push forward in future. The most successful business owners in the world adopt a mature approach to building up their businesses and have people with the right ideas and perspectives at the helm of affairs. They realise what makes a business great and structure it in the way other successful and enduring businesses are modelled.

A good business model does not just focus solely on the output the business generates. Instead, the business model addresses key issues like:

- the business process and how it works, instead of the projects the business has to accomplish
- how profitable the business can be, rather than how the sales revenue will come into place

- where the business is going in future, instead of how the current reality can be repeated multiple times
- how the business operates on the whole, instead of the roles of the separate parts of the business
- what the business's future will be, rather than focusing on the model that is currently in use.

The artist model often comes to the limelight in the maturity stage. In the artist model, providing what customers need based on different demographical classifications is the major focus. Other competitors also get focused on, to figure out what makes them tick.

Deciding on what the business structure needs to be if the customers' needs are to be met is also a priority and takes up attention and time.

At this point, the business is now the coming together of various parts and features, all focused towards achieving a goal. Standards, operating rules, and corporate principles are set and start to see adoption. Here a clearly structured system that is easily duplicated then emerges.

Here the customer is seen not as a stick tossed in the wheel of the artist, stopping them from doing what they want, but as an asset deserving of the value being produced.

In summary, a business attains maturity stage at the point where the customer becomes the focus, as opposed to the service or product being at the centre stage. Here the process of conducting business is more important than the business that is being conducted.

However, this can only happen if the business model in use is balanced and allows the artist, the manager, and the technician the opportunity to contribute positively to the process of building the business.

Let's quickly recap what we have discovered so far:

1. Change is external, and transformation is internal. Transformation can let you see the limitation of the change which a person cannot see.
2. A business needs all three personnel types to function properly: an artist, a manager, and a technician.
3. All three types of personnel are essential for the business. They are similar to different parts of a vehicle combining to make the vehicle functional and make the whole journey enjoyable.
4. A business has three stages: infancy, expansion, and maturity. Each stage of business has a different priority.
5. As a business owner, you should always be aware of whatever stage your business is currently in and the point where you plan to make an exit. How you exit the business is as important as how you enter the business.

It is time to create your own unique business identity. Knowing is not enough; we must take action. How many times have you felt like you have discovered something valuable, but you never put it into practice? Why? Because intellectually you know what you have learnt is valuable, but until you write down all the thoughts on paper and take consistent action, your new-found knowledge will remain just a nice idea. Knowledge is not power; knowledge is potential power. Once you put the knowledge to work, you will create your own unique experience. You have an understanding of the aspects of the business that work and the parts that don't. Now you have the wisdom. Your wisdom will guide you through the doubt and uncertainty. Your wisdom will give you the practical power to overcome the challenges ahead.

Take a moment to think about the questions below and write down your answers. Don't look for perfection in your answers; whatever thoughts that first come into your mind are the right answers.

1. Am I an entrepreneur, a manager, or a technician? (Remember that you could be a mix of all these roles; it is more about which role you are better at playing.)
2. Which role has been my comfort zone, and which are not getting filled enough? For that matter, what roles have I totally neglected, and how can I acquire them?
3. What skills or tools do I need to learn (or hire) to help me overcome the obvious obstacles that are restricting my growth, sales, and profitability?
4. Which areas of my business could be delegated or outsourced to someone else to free me up to do the things that would add the most value?
5. What stage is my business in right now, and what should be my priority for this stage?
6. What type of business is mine going to be? How can I take steps to transform my current business into the future business I want it to be?

CHAPTER FOUR

Principle 4
Improvise. Adapt. Overcome.

Have you ever played video games with your kids or nephews? My sister has three teenage boys, so one of my favourite things to do on Sunday afternoons is to spend time with my three nephews. As you can almost rightly guess, one of their favourite activities when I'm around is playing the Xbox. I'm bad at playing games on the Xbox, so I usually tell them that I'm not into video games. This often results in them nagging me and saying, 'Come on, Uncle, just one game, just one!'

In the end, I usually say, 'All right, all right, let's just play one game.'

Unlike me, my nephews are masters in these games. A bit of 'Phew, phew, phew!' and I'm usually dead within a minute or two of the game, while they still keep going for at least forty-five more minutes. I often find myself asking, 'How do these little kids manage to beat me every time we play video games? Are they smarter than I am? Are they more knowledgeable about video games? Or are they just naturally gifted?' The answer to these questions is clearly no.

So why are they so good at video games?

The secret is one word—*anticipation*. My nephews have been playing these video games for so long that they are able to anticipate what comes next in the game. Instead of reacting to sudden gunfire from the game, they are fully prepared for the surprise and act accordingly. I, on the other hand, was in full react mode because I had never played these games and didn't have an idea of what was ahead.

Business is just like playing this video game. It occurs in a fast-moving environment with lots of uncertainty. In business, you can't always anticipate or predict what will happen next, so you're often stuck reacting to issues instead of acting in advance. This is very tiring and draining because you are working against the natural law of the business cycle. Here you are relying on trial and error to work out how the business survives. It is similar to how farmers need to anticipate the seasons ahead. They understand that there are four seasons of the year, and they can plant in spring and harvest in the autumn. It is simple pattern recognition. Pattern recognition is a critical and powerful instinct we inherited from our ancestors. If we know how to apply this anticipation in the business, it can allow us to work with the market instead of against the market. Using our instinctive pattern recognition can empower us to make intelligent and calculated risks.

Successful entrepreneurs think like farmers. They anticipate what is coming in the market trends.

A lot of us assume that successful entrepreneurs take giant, almost impossible risks so as to get large financial returns. This, however, is not true. In the past five years, I have worked closely with some of the nation's foremost entrepreneurs, especially in technology start-ups, such as realestate.com and saleezy.com, and defence force entrepreneurs (Safety Direct Solutions and RSM Transport). Having been immersed in the operations of these successful start-ups, I have seen a pattern of why those business owners are more resilient compared with other start-ups: they anticipate what is coming. They actively protect their downside risk and ensure they have safeguards in time for the anticipated winter seasons.

One quote from the founder of Alibaba, Jack Ma, has summarised it quite well: 'You don't fix your roof in the raining season. You fix your roof on sunny days so you can have the peace of mind to enjoy the winter.' Warren Buffet also said it well: 'Rule no. 1: never lose money. Rule no. 2: never forget rule no. 1.'

If you make a 50 per cent loss on an investment, you need to make a 100 per cent gain just to break even. This is why it is so critical to plan carefully and execute wisely. Learning how to protect your downside risk while optimising your upside returns is what this chapter is about.

You may say, 'Lincoln, no risk, no reward. You have to take risks to gain the rewards.' Yes, you are right. Business does require taking risks, but it takes calculated risks. Ask yourself: What is the worst-case scenario that could occur regarding the business ideas I am about to kick-start? Am I fully prepared to take this loss? What would be the upside gain? Does the upside gain far exceed the possible downside loss?

Two powerful distinctions which will be made in this chapter are going to help you uncover the secrets of successful businesses: how these business owners anticipate the market and reduce the uncertainty that exists in the volatile business environment.

Distinction #1
Design Your Way to Success

I am going to share with you a cutting-edge business thinking process called design thinking. This cutting-edge strategy could effectively improve your success rate by over 200 per cent. I learnt this entire thinking process from the Harvard Business School.

Some years ago, I came across a news article that stated that Harvard Business School had produced more successful CEOs than all other business schools in the whole world put together. I'm always passionate about personal development, and I believe that while formal education can make you a living, self-education can make you a fortune. So I signed up for an executive education program at Harvard, hoping that I would be able to improve my business. To my surprise, the program was one of the best, most value-adding programs I had ever come across. I not only met so many wonderful business people in the cohort, but I also learnt the entire design thinking process, which helped me and my business boost revenue to over 200 per cent in the following nine months. Every time you come close to giving up, just think about how *you are just one idea away from doubling your income. If you are not earning, make sure you are learning.*

First, what is this design thinking I speak of? How can you use it in your business to help you achieve business success?

Design thinking is the same philosophy that designers apply when trying to design a table or a desk. They need to go through multiple phases of refining and redesigning until the final version of the product emerges. By applying the designer's mentality to design our future business, there will be no failure, as everything plays a part in the process. Also, design thinking allows us to avoid having a 'need to be perfect to start' mentality, as it is all about end users—our future customers. Design thinking puts the human first. It begins with empathising with a real person—your prospect, your customer, your partner, or whoever you are designing for—feeling their pain and putting yourself in their shoes and understanding what they are going through.

Design thinking is not a linear process; it is a mindset, a way of thinking. People want to be cared about and thought of. They not only want to *hear* your story, but they also want to *be in* your story. The new mantra is 'Don't show me. Involve me.'

Design thinking shifts our mindset from traditional self-focus to end-user (customer) focus. For example, I always believed that in order to achieve my goal, I needed to pursue more degrees, read more books, and attend more seminars. I always focused on myself. I never understood the fact that in business, the focus should be on the clients. What challenges do they have? Why do they buy my product and service? What problems do they have that I have a solution to? How can I help them better overcome their challenges compared with other service providers? How can I provide more value?

Once I shifted my focus from myself to my client, the entire business started to work like it was magic. People come from everywhere to support my mission; my clients drive two hours to see me for thirty-minute appointments. Why? Because they saw me as the go-to guy for the solutions they needed. They realised that I had the answers to help them overcome their challenge.

Powerful stuff, right? This is design thinking. This unique thinking methodology helps you transform your focus from the inside out.

One more example: this book you are reading now, *Thrive*, is a product of design thinking.

I wrote this book based entirely on the design thinking process. I've always been passionate about teaching, and I have been teaching and mentoring over the past ten years. My students are all over, from high school students to university students. However, I hesitated to write a book because I knew it might take a while to finish up. Also, writing is not one of my strongest skills (my brain was making up excuses when I was thinking about how to be perfect). By applying design thinking, I was able to start this book and had the confidence that this book could definitely create a lot of value for future readers. You might be wondering how exactly design thinking applied here. Here's how:

I. I started the draft version instead of thinking I needed to write one perfect final copy. I realised that writing a book involves a lot of editing and changes between the first edition and the final copy, but it does not matter. It is like applying the designers' mindset; it is a work in progress between the final products.

With this, I felt more freedom to write down the ideas in my head. My entire attention was shifted from how to be perfect on the first go to forming the basic ideas and writing with a flow.

II. I had a purpose right from the very beginning: This book is going to be a guide for people who want to take control of their finance. This book is going to teach people how to be business owners, not just operators. This book is going to serve future readers; it is going to help solve the business challenges that they are going to face. In other words, I put the readers' needs first. The book provides solutions for the problems in the current market.

III. I was always seeking feedback from the readers of the draft version and marketing the book even before it had been released. Writing the book is only 50 per cent of the work; figuring out how to market and distribute it to future readers is the other 50 per cent of the work.

By applying designers' mindset, we can align our vision and actionable strategies into work. We are no longer waiting for the perfect answers, and instead we work towards refining our product for the customer. This process can be likened to baking a cupcake. The whole process and all the ingredients are working towards reaching the final version. One good thing is that you are confident that your cupcakes will sell, because you have produced them based on what the customers want.

Let's break down design thinking into five simple steps and put them into business practice context:

Design Thinking Process

Empathize — Learn about your audience
Define — Construct point of view based on user needs
Ideate — Brainstorm and come up with creative solutions
Prototype — Build representation
Test — Test your ideas

One of my good friends, Heidi, wanted to start a home pie-making business. She already had a substantial amount of experience and passion for making pies over the years, but she still did not know how to start. She was uncertain whether her passion for making pies could actually attract enough customers to make it a worthwhile business venture. Also, she didn't have enough capital to invest in her initial business start-up. We started our work together using five steps to help establish the business.

Step 1. Empathise

> Seek first to understand, then to be understood.
>
> Stephen Covey

I started the business consultancy with Heidi to find out who our first clients would be. I say *client* on purpose, as opposed to *customer*, as customers usually have one-time relationships with the business. Clients have lifetime value because we can carry out repeat businesses with them. Replacing the word *client* with the word *customer* can help you think about potential long-term relationships in your daily business transactions. Apple Inc. strategically considers every customer who buys their computers their long-term clients instead of just customers. They constantly try to create different ideas and products to fulfil the clients' needs, such as the Apple watch, iPad, and iPhone.

> Happy customers will leave you if they find a cheaper deal, but fulfilled clients will become your raving fans and will stay with your business through thick and thin.

We covered the following questions. I suggest you go through the same questions with the business ideas you have.

1. Who are your potential customers?
2. What current problems do they have with the products you are offering now?
3. Can you describe a whole day of your ideal customers? What does their lifestyle look like?

To gain a better understanding of our clients, we need to learn about them, and to do this, we use a tool called client journey mapping.

A client journey map (CJM) is a useful tool in design thinking that can help you gain better insight into how target clients respond to certain products and service lines. A CJM is a very straightforward idea; it is a diagrammatic representation of the steps a client goes through when engaging with a company, whether it be purchasing a product, an online experience, retail experience, a service, or any combination of these client interfaces. The CJM is used for understanding and addressing client needs and pain points.

In its most basic form, journey mapping begins by compiling a series of user goals and actions into a timeline skeleton. Next, the skeleton is fleshed out with user thoughts and emotions to create a narrative. Finally, that story is condensed into a visualisation that is used to communicate insights that will advise the design processes.

The more touchpoints the map has, the more complicated it becomes. There are four elements that inform a client's journey map:

- *Actions*. What is the client doing at each stage? What actions are they taking to move themselves on to the next level? Seek the answers from the client's point of view instead of the company's perspective.

- *Motivations.* What is the motive of the client, and what are the actions required for them to go to the next stage? What emotions are they seeking? Why do they care about your company offer?
- *Questions.* What are the uncertainties, jargon, or other issues preventing the client from moving to the next stage?
- *Barriers.* What structure, process, cost, implementation, or other obstacles stand in the client's way of moving on to the next level?

Step 2. Define

Defining specifically addresses the current challenges that clients face when they buy similar products in the market. It uncovers the problem we are solving. Business is all about solving problems; the clearer the problem we are finding a solution to, the easier it is to provide these needed solutions.

Brook and I went on to define the following questions:

1. What future customers' needs to create the pie?
2. What is the current gap in the market?
3. Is there a need in the market today for pies?
4. Why is Brook's pie a better option for future clients?

Step 3. Ideate

After understanding the limitations of the existing products and services, the next stage in the design thinking process is called ideating.

The ideating stage is an all-ideas-are-welcome stage, and no idea is exempt. The point here isn't to pick the good ideas out of the bad ones or to find that one best solution; it is to bring out as many possibilities as possible. One defining feature of the ideating stage is that it pushes for collaboration and participation. The defining point here is that everyone has a creative part to them, so the ideating stage and its brainstorming process can seek solutions from different minds and perspectives all focused on resolving the same issues, thus having the advantage of the different mindsets and perspectives.

> What possible ideas do you have to close the gap between what your customer wants and what things they need so we can market what they want and sell what they need?

Wants are not the same as needs. In making pies, for example, while future clients want the feeling of being cared for and eating healthy after purchasing the pie, what they actually need is pie that is freshly baked and made with good ingredients. We can then market what the clients want (good health and happiness) and deliver what they need (fresh home-made pies).

Step 4. Prototype

The process of creating a prototype usually helps clear up the problem and provides new perspectives to the problem and possible solutions that may have been ignored. When preparing to proceed to the last stage, prototypes that can be tried by your audience are always helpful in gathering feedback. The prototype stage enables us to put the brainstormed ideas into a practical real-world environment, without significant initial cost. Instantaneous feedback based on the experiment helps identify the best solution for both the company and the client. Can you make a sample product or a simple landing web page? Without too much investment required upfront, create a sample that captures all the features of the product you are going to offer to the customers.

Step 5. Test

Instead of her buying a brand-new oven, I suggested to Brook that she make the first pie sample at home and share the pie with dozens of her friends and ask them for two particular actionable items:

1. give feedback on the pie
2. refer the pie to other possibly interested friends.

If each of her friends had referred 10 other friends to have a taste of Brook's pie, this equalled 10 × 10 = 100 new pie customers before we even began the business, and we also got real-time feedback from the potential clients. Exciting stuff, am I right? We are just getting started.

Share the sample with potential clients and seek their feedback. Many start-ups in the financial services sector begin with an interesting idea for a product that they think people will want. They then spend months, sometimes years, perfecting that product without ever showcasing and prototyping it, even in a very primitive form, to prospective customers. When they fail to reach the mass target customers, it is often because of the lack of communication with potential clients to determine whether the product is exciting for them.

Deploying the minimum viable product (MVP) concept from design thinking could assist the breakthrough point for the start-up. A core component of MVP methodology is the construction of a 'build, measure, learn' feedback loop. The MVP methodology should be implemented at every stage of product development so that the feedback from targeted customers is inbuilt in the final products.

The MVP method adopts the perspective that every start-up is a form of grand experiment that attempts to answer a question. The key question, however, is not 'Can this product be built?' Instead, the question becomes 'Should this product be built?' and 'Can we build a sustainable business around this set of goods and services?'

Critically, these experiments are not just theoretical or conceptual. If the MVP is successful, it allows a manager to push on with their proposal—enlisting early adopters, adding employees to each further experiment, and ultimately, starting to build a product. By the time the product is finalised for retail, it will already have established customers. It will have already solved some real problems it was created to solve and will thus have established detailed specifications for what needs to be built.

With this step, you can already know who your clients are or will be before you even have the business up and running. Your clients here already have first-hand experience with the products and services you're offering. When this is accomplished, who will be your first client and customer? The clients you have reached out to already, because your products were made based on what their needs are.

Let's quickly recap what we have learnt so far:

1. Design thinking is a process that lets you focus on the end users and solve the problems that people are willing to pay for.
2. A lot of times, when we try to start a business, fear of the unknown is often the main factor that stops people from taking the first step. Design thinking changes our perception of failure by considering all the outcomes as part of the work process.
3. Shifting your focus from your own ideology to that of serving the customer and building your entire business for the singular purpose of serving your prospective clients are the core of design thinking.

Design thinking gives you a powerful framework with which to accelerate your business engine, but how do you ensure that this vehicle is heading in the right direction? The direction not only empowers you, but it also attracts others to your mission.

The second distinction and the three purpose circles (TPC) will help you uncover your direction.

Distinction #2
Align Your Passion with Your Business

Don't just busy to make a living, design a life.

Jim Rohn

With design thinking as our framework, we can now design a workable business machine that the market is willing to pay for. But how can we align the business we create with our highest purpose?

Quite often, I've had career gurus give me advice like 'Quit your job and follow your passion'.

However, I don't completely agree with this statement. I agree that you should work for the job you love and should not waste your time on a job that you feel is draining your talent. However, most people don't even know what jobs actually make them feel fulfilled, so they play the game of trial and error. Hopefully, they get it right one day.

I believe every job is designed based on its functionality. Jobs are not meant to make us feel fulfilled. The job itself has absolutely no meaning, but we give meaning to the job.

For example, I used to work in a fast-food restaurant, flipping burgers to earn a living to pass through my college. At the beginning, I honestly hated the job; it had low pay and high demand, and it was highly repetitive on the same tasks.

See, I attached a negative meaning to the actions of the job, so I put my job in a negative context.

One day, I told myself, 'Look, Lincoln, I know you don't like this job. I get it. But this job at least pays for your rent and food. You should be grateful for it. You can do your best in the job and still seek other opportunities that align more with your potential.'

So I changed my attitude to the job, and my manager was really surprised about why I was so happy on every shift. Just after three months, I was promoted to be the store manager, and I got the chance to learn the whole franchise operation at the company's head office. This experience served me very well later in my own business development.

The point of this story is that you don't have to love whatever job you're doing right now; you just need to think of it as a tool you need so you can climb the career ladder. When you are climbing the steepest mountain of your career, would you still complain about your tools? I doubt so. You will love every tool you have, as they are necessary for your survival in this journey.

Chasing your passion is dangerous advice for any business.

In business, relying solely on your passion to start the business is like riding a bike with one wheel. There is a very high chance that you might fail.

Think about it. Passion may be the reason you started your business, but the market doesn't care for your passion. The clients want their problems solved in an efficient way. Passion may be an essential factor for successful businesses, but it is not *all* the required elements to build a successful business.

Let me share with you the three purpose circles (TPC) I usual display in my seminars to help my clients get a crystal-clear vision of what they want to create.

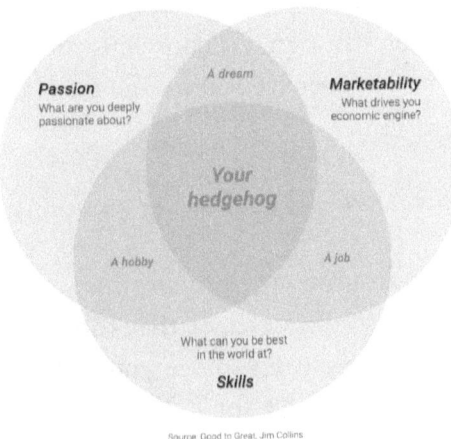

Source: Good to Great, Jim Collins

Imagine your future business or ideal job is a combination of these three circles:

1. what you are passionate about
2. the skills you have mastered
3. the skills the current market is willing to pay for.

Passion

The things you are deeply passionate about can change over time, which is why we need to have self-awareness: What drives me to perform better? What am I excited about for the next few years? The clearer and more honest you are with yourself, the better the vision you have of yourself will be. These questions are fascinating ones. Some people are immediately aware of their interests and get very excited when they tell you about it, but most people have no idea what they are interested in! They say things like 'I don't know' and 'I am not passionate about anything'. Why aren't people aware of their passions?

Passions are feelings or emotions that cause our attention to be focused on something. Interests are a function of the limbic system and not of conscious, logical thought, hence why most people aren't aware of them.

Because interest is provided by the limbic system, we may be unable to access this information through our conscious thoughts. Alternatively, we need to look at how we behave and see the things that attract us and the things that repel us.

How do we do that? Answer the following questions:

1. What's your favourite movie of all time?
2. Who is the main character of that movie? Chances are, you like that movie because you see yourself most like the main character. Search Google for 'XX character analysis' and read up on this character.
3. Go to your YouTube viewing history and scroll through the videos you've been watching. What general trends/patterns do you see there?
4. Ask your girlfriend, wife, or best friend what the things you don't shut up about are. They will know this better than you, so you should ask them!
5. What books have you read from cover to cover? Look at your collection and sort the books you've read from cover to cover and then ask yourself what trends/patterns these have in common.
6. Where does your money go? Look at your bank statements over the past thirty, sixty, ninety days and see what you've been spending money on. What general patterns/trends do you see there? Where attention goes, energy flows! Discover where your energy (time and money) is flowing, and you'll discover what you're interested in.

Your passions are the most powerful forces inside you, and they matter more than your cognitive ability. Somebody with passion and interest will dominate somebody with more intelligence and less interest. If you haven't found your thing yet, keep looking! When you find it, you'll find the fire.

Talent

Talent refers to the skills you have mastered. In the book *Outliers*, author Malcolm Gladwell states that in order to master any skill, you need at least ten thousand hours of dedicated study and improvement. That is equal to seven to ten years of practicing and refining your craft. That is why finding your passion is so important. Otherwise, you will spend so much time devoted to learning and training to be an expert in your field for the things you do not like. Remember, success and mastery are relative. For example, I feel extremely confident with my mathematic skills because I have been practicing it for the past two decades. I have been taught math in various disciplines over the past eight years. However, if I compare my math skills with my university professors', I would never think of getting into teaching. So be confident; the areas where your talents lie could be relatively simple, like cooking, storytelling, fitness, painting, or horse riding.

Money

Money refers to the price the current market is willing to pay for the products or service you are offering. Apply the design thinking framework we talked about in distinction #1 of this chapter to guide you towards the right pathway. The crucial part of this thinking framework is to create a valuable product that clients need and are willing to pay for.

Let me share a couple of success stories my clients made in their business by applying the three purpose circles.

Success Case 1

One of my clients, Andrew, started his first business—running a weekend fitness boot camp. We used the three purpose circles to verify his business ideas.

Talent: Andrew has been undergoing strength and condition training over the past decade, and he has sustainable knowledge in the field to help others improve their fitness and wellness in a short period.

Passion: Andrew is very passionate about fitness, and he has mastered the physical movement. He also has a strong passion to share his knowledge with others.

Money: Soon after Andrew and I went through the design thinking process stated in this chapter, he discovered that prospective clients wanted to get proven results via his fitness system, and they saw these solutions as something that was worth spending on.

Success Case 2

Another example is a business start-up with my client Tracey. Tracey wanted to start organising dating events.

Money: She founded the business venture because she saw that people who had just emigrated from countries overseas to Australia needed to build a network and find their future partners, and she saw that they considered this service to be valuable enough to pay for.

Talent: Having been an event manager for over seven years, Tracey was a master at networking, and she was well trained and equipped to deliver an unforgettable experience for the guests.

Passion: Tracy was also very passionate about helping clients connect with their future partners, as it was fun and rewarding for her to see couples she brought together get married.

It was a very successful business, and her events got eleven couples married within three years! It beats online dating any time.

At this point, you may have concerns and questions like 'Lincoln, what if I find my business idea, but it is still not working?'

That is a very good question, so let's think about it this way: How long will it take your child to learn how to walk? Until you shut him off.

You might reply, 'That is a dumb question, Lincoln. My child will be able to walk for as long as it takes!'

That is correct, and it explains why the world is filled with people who are able to walk around. The magic answer for what we want to succeed in is this: For as long as it takes, don't stop trying until you achieve your goals. Change your approach; if one way is not working, try the other one. It is not about the resources you have; it is about being resourceful.

I would encourage you to take a break from this book now and take a moment to answer the following questions, which can help you clarify your thinking process:

1. What financial goals do you want to accomplish in the course of the next ten years?
2. Why these goals? Who will feel the impact?
3. What actions can you take now to get the very first step started?

Time to create your unique business DNA. List down your answers to the following three questions:

1. What areas are you deeply passionate about? What are the jobs you are willing to do 24/7 without getting paid?
2. What are your key skills that you are most confident in?
3. Are there people ready to pay for this service or product?

CHAPTER FIVE

Principle 5
Visualise the Compelling Future

Where there is no vision, the people perish; but he that keepeth the law, happy is he.

The Bible

'Would you tell me, please, which way I ought to go from here?'
'That depends a good deal on where you want to get to,' said the Cat.
'I don't much care where,' said Alice.
'Then it doesn't matter which way you go,' said the Cat.

Alice's classic encounter with the Cheshire Cat in Lewis Carroll's *Alice's Adventures in Wonderland* reveals the close connection between vision and choice. Live with a vision, and you will know where to go. Live by choice, and you will know what you have to do to get you there.

When each day begins, we each have a choice. We can ask 'What shall I do?' or 'What should I do?' Without direction, without purpose, whatever you *shall do* will always get you somewhere. But when you're going somewhere based on the vision you've created, there will always be something you *should do* that will get you where you must go.

Imagine you are driving 100 kilometres per hour at night on a strange road and have no idea where you are. There are no lights on the road, and the only thing you can see is 100 metres in front of you, which is as far as your car's headlights can let you see. All you can see is the 100 metres ahead, and the only other guide you have is the voice from your car's GPS navigation system. Do you feel lost? You would probably say no. Why? It is because you trust the GPS, and you trust your instinct. You may say to yourself, 'If I can handle the 100 metres ahead of me, I can handle the next 200 kilometres with ease. I just need to follow the directions well, 100 metres after 100 metres, and in the end, I will be fine.' This is faith. Faith is trust in something you cannot see.

This same principle applies to building a successful business. You start the journey by imagining the compelling future of your business. Business, I believe, is a spiritual journey. The modern company framework follows traditional church organisational structure: In the church, the pastor preaches what he believes in, i.e. God and Jesus, and that all the faithful followers in the religion will be rewarded with a peaceful life and unlimited prosperity in the future. Church attendees voluntarily follow the pastor only if they believe in the vision he shares. In most countries, no one forces you to go to church; you have no obligation to go to church. Most people who choose to attend the regular Sunday service do so because they believe in the vision of what the pastor shares. In other words, church attendees go to church voluntarily. People follow the pastor not because of his position and power within the organisation but because of the power of his vision.

When people respect you as a person, they admire you.
When they respect you as a friend, they love you. When they respect you as a leader, they follow you.

This is why the church is one of the best places to develop leadership skills.

So let's examine the modern company structure. It follows a similar pattern to that of the church: The business founder has a business idea, which he starts to share with everyone around him. The customers will purchase the product only if they believe in the value the product offers them. The company's employees will devote their time and talent to work for this business idea only if they can see the common vision ahead. As such, building a successful company requires a tremendous amount of leadership.

Your customers follow your vision voluntarily, and they do this by purchasing your products. Keep in mind, they can always choose other products, but if they believe in your values and follow your vision, they are more likely to choose your products.

Your employees follow your vision voluntarily, and they do this by contributing their time and talent to your company. You can pay them to come to work, but you can't pay their heart and soul to follow your vision.

Your investors also follow your vision voluntarily, and they do this by contributing their resources (money and expertise) to your business venture. Remember that they can choose other companies to invest in.

The key to building a successful company is having an unshakeable and compelling vision. A vision that not only prompts you to start the business but also allows other people to sign up as part of the business's future. Being able to effectively align your business with your vision is what this chapter is about.

The three distinctions in this chapter are going to empower you to turn what you have envisioned into possibilities. You will not only be focused on building a business, but you will also have the strength to do more, give more, and become more every day.

Distinction #1
How to Turn Nothing into Something

Thirteen years ago, I worked fifty plus hours in a fast-food company. Week after week, my biggest goal was to afford my gas and grocery bills. I gave myself lots of excuses for everything I didn't have: job opportunities, permanent residence (equivalent to the green card in the US), and even my Chinese accent. I still remember every night, after twelve-hour shifts, I liked to sit in the car and listen to Tony Robbins' self-improvement tape for hours and think, *There is something more out there, but I really don't know how I can get started.*

I always dreamed of travelling around the world while having the freedom of choice to share my knowledge with others in the same journey of creating their dream. This dream became so clear that I couldn't even go to sleep at night without thinking about it. However, the fear of putting my ideas out there and everything that could possibly come after always held me back. I was so afraid to even share my dreams with my friends because I thought they would see it in a negative light, that they would judge me or make fun of me, and that they would think I was arrogant.

I often told myself, 'What if this happened? And on top of that, this other thing happened? I would be better off not trying at all. I can always be safe if I do not try at all.'

Until one day, I was so disappointed with myself for not making progress towards the goals I had, because of my fear.

I told myself, 'Look, Lincoln, you may prefer safety and security, and that is perfectly fine. You could just stay in a corner, quiet and safe. You could wait for someone to protect you, for someone to give you food and shelter. You could hold all your dreams and desires within you. Don't share with anyone, and you could probably live till you are 100 years old. But is that really the way you want to live?'

'No, that is not how I want to live. It is better to live 30 years with adventure than live 100 years in safety and security. Why am I so concerned with how others think about me? It is not what they think about me that determines what I can do. It is how I think about myself that shapes my destiny. Lincoln, starting a business is risky, investing in real estate is risky, and staying with your current employer is also risky. You are too afraid to face your challenge,' I told myself without an iota of doubt in my mind.

Don't ask for safe and secure; ask for more adventure. It is all risky. The minute we were born was when life became risky. If you think trying is risky, wait till they give you the bill for not trying. If you think investing is risky, wait till you start to regret not investing. Getting married is risky, having a child is risky, and going into business to face uncertainty is risky. It is all risky. Want to know how risky life is? You won't be getting out of life alive—no one will. That is risky. The only way you'll know how things will work out is if you give it a shot.

From that day onwards, I started to take actions towards my goals: building a business website, marketing my business, reading over seven hundred books in the areas of business and psychology, attending various seminars to build my skills, and joining Toastmasters to improve my public speaking skills. If there was anything in my head that I felt scared about, I did it immediately. Your determination and willpower is like a muscle; the more often you use it, the stronger it will become.

Fast-forward to ten years later, the businesses I build allow me to work with amazing people and travel across the world to any destination, which I had never dreamed of before. If you had told me ten years ago that all these things were going to happen to me, I would have said, 'Be realistic.'

Realistic? Why should you be realistic? Be wiser. The only thing standing between you and your goal is the false story you keep telling yourself as to why you can't achieve it. If you can change, everything else will change for you.

The more I reflect on the journey, the better I start to understand the process of how to turn nothing into something.

Now what do you have to do to turn nothing into something?

I. First, to turn nothing into something, you have to begin with some ideas and imagination.

Now calling ideas and imagination 'nothing' may be difficult, but in truth, how tangible are these ideas? It's a mystery. Personally, I don't believe that ideas that can become big businesses and corporations or vaccines or a trip to the moon should be classified as nothing. However, you do not have anything tangible yet.

If you think about it, ideas are so powerful that to your consciousness, they start to seem real even before something tangible comes out of them. Imagination can be so strong that you can see what you are imagining.

Now it might be hard to call ideas and imagination nothing, but how tangible are those ideas? That is a bit of a mystery. I don't believe that ideas that can be turned into a hotel, ideas that can be turned into an enterprise, ideas that can be turned into a new vaccine, or ideas that can be turned into some miracle product should be called nothing. But tangibly, you have nothing.

Interesting! Think of it: ideas that become so powerful in your mind and in your consciousness that they seem real to you even before they become tangible. Imagination that is so strong you can actually see it.

We are a special kind of species on this planet. We create everything *twice*. The first time, we create the imagination in our head, and the second time, we make it tangible. Think about how we build a house: We ask an architect to design and draft the house, laying out the car garage, study room, kitchen, bathroom, etc. All these need to be done before we even lay the first brick.

So the first thing to do when trying to turn nothing into something is to *imagine the possibilities*. Imagine *all* that could possibly happen. This is why seminars, sermons, and testimonials from other people exist—to show us that anything is possible and to help us imagine and see the potential.

II. Now the second step for transforming nothing into something is that you must *believe* that the things you imagine are possible for you.

Testimonials like 'If I can do it, you can do it' soon become a foundation for our own beliefs, and eventually, we start to believe them. We first imagine that it is possible, then we start to believe that if it can happen to other people, it is also possible for us.

You can also start to believe in what you are doing based on what you have done before. Your testimonial could say, 'If I did it once, I can do it again. If it happened for me before, it could very well happen again.'

So we first believe what other people say. 'If I can do it, you can do it. If I can change, you can change. If I can start with nothing, you can start with nothing. If I can turn it all around, you can turn it all around.' Then we back this up with our own testimonies from something we have done in the past. 'If we did it once, we can do it again. If we did it last year, we can do it this year.' Combining these two testimonials can be very powerful. Now although we do not have actual substance yet, we are very close to one already.

When I started my very first business, I talked to many of my mentors who had started their own successful businesses, and I listened to their experiences and testimonials. They shared with me how they overcame uncertainty and how they dealt with the challenges that came along in the course of the journey. It gave me a substantial amount of confidence. If they could do it, I believed I had a fair chance of achieving my goals as well.

Again, the first step is to imagine all that can be possible. The second step is to imagine that all that you think is possible is also possible for you. Step two here can be described simply as faith to believe.

A writer once stated that 'faith is the substance'. An interesting word: *substance*. The ability to see the things that are possible and see them as also being possible for you. If you can believe, then your faith has substance, which is a piece of something tangible. While it is not the real thing, it is powerful enough in your mind that it is close to the real thing. The writer also described faith as evidence—substance and evidence. Substance and evidence cannot just be dismissed as 'nothing'. While it cannot yet be seen by the physical eyes, a person with faith can see it already. Although it is not yet tangible, your ideas and dreams can become something if you have faith that it is something. In this case, the substance and evidence that you have eventually becomes powerful enough that it can be transformed into something real.

> III. The last step is to model someone who has done it before and to take a massive amount of action to achieve your goal.

Success leaves clues. Think: What is the fastest way to solve a math question? Follow a proven formula. Instead of reinventing the entire formula, you can follow the success formula and get the same result over and over again. If anyone records constant success at anything, it is not because they're lucky. There are some behaviours, beliefs, values, and actions that allow these people to produce remarkable results frequently. We all have similar minds, so we can also record these types of results if we learn how they are achieving them. The fastest way to succeed and transform ourselves is to *model* ourselves after these people.

By modelling yourself after successful people, you can squeeze years of experience into days and weeks, so you can quicken your growth. Sadly, a lot of people do not know how they can model success or what it involves. When I'm trying to replicate success, I refer to Robert Dilts's six Logical Levels.

This principle says that any change to anything must align with the following levels in order:

- environment
- behaviour
- capabilities
- beliefs/values
- identity
- spiritual/vision.

If you are trying to model a successful person, you need to know what their internal and external process is at each of these levels.

If you do this well enough, you can be successful much faster than if you don't do it.

A lot of people attempt to copy behaviours and actions without realising that modelling the higher levels (spiritual, identity, beliefs/values) is a lot more important. The diagram below illustrates the fundamentals of modelling:

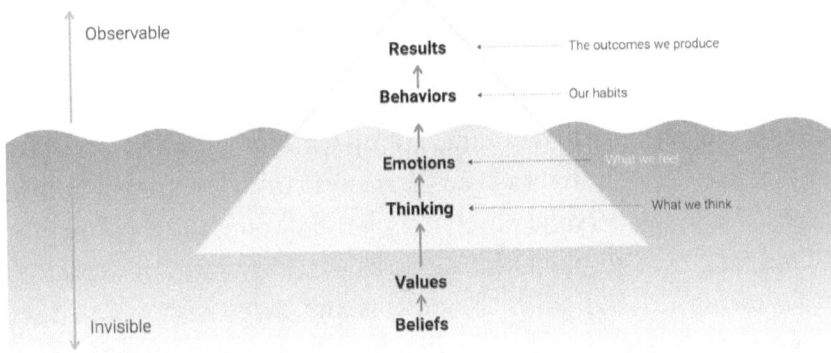

You see, our values and beliefs determine what actions to take. This is why I consider working with your mindset as well as the other levels to be very important; it can help you become successful much faster.

As much as you can, try to use the experiences of people that are more successful than you as a guideline.

Once you know which model to follow, the rest is all about taking committed action.

Action is the process of making your ideas tangible. It is like building a house. Once the architect has designed the house's blueprint, all the builder needs to do is physically build the house brick by brick.

What if you took action but still have not achieved your outcome? Change your approach. Imagine I said to you, 'How long will it take your child to learn how to walk? Until you shut him off and ask him not to try any more.' You would say, 'Are you crazy? My kid will learn to walk as long as it takes.' Magic formula: try a different approach for as long as it takes till you achieve your goals.

Distinction #2
Begin with Why

In the Bible, there is the quote 'Ask, and you shall receive'. I believe asking is the key part of receiving. In my seminar, when I asked, 'How many of you have written a New Year's resolution but never followed through?' almost everyone raised their hands. Some audience members told me they even stopped writing goals years ago, as they are tired of not following through with the process and being disappointed with the outcome. Why do we believe that we have to come up with a list of goals we want to achieve every year? Why can't we follow through with these goals? The answer is, you don't have enough reasons for doing what you do now.

For example, if you are trying to lose excess weight so you can be healthy again, you may set SMART (specific, measurable, achievable, relevant, and time-based) goals. You want to lose three kilograms in the next six weeks. You are going to the gym five times a week and eating six small high-protein and low-carb meals throughout the day.

Does this action plan motivate you? Yeah, you're motivated for the first few days or even the first week. There is one ingredient missing in the plan, however: your reason for setting and pursuing these goals. Why do you want to lose weight? Why three kilograms? Compelling reasons like this: once you are healthy again, you will be able to fit into your dress, be more confident, and date the person you have always dreamt of. The compelling future could make all the difference.

You make progress either through inspiration or desperation. Motivational forces exist in two forms: push and pull. Push is necessary at the beginning, but it is exhausting in the long term. You push yourself to go to the gym, start a new diet, or follow the financial goals you have set. The push power will give you momentum at the beginning, but you will have diminishing rate of returns after a while, as willpower will not always be available to you. Pull power, on the other hand, has a long-lasting effect. Your vision pulls you to go through the difficulty; your *why* pulls you to overcome the challenges in the business. If your *why* is strong enough, your *how* will get easier.

I recall when I was a child, every Friday, I would sit through a two-hour bus ride to stay over at my grandma's house for the weekend. Before I would head to the bus stop, my mum would usually tell me the agenda for the whole weekend, and I would either feel excited or very upset depending on whether I liked the agenda or not. If she told me, 'Lincoln, you have an English test coming up, so you need to spend the whole weekend studying,' I would totally flat out during the two-hour bus ride and imagine what the weekend would be like with ten English books. If Mum told me, 'Lincoln, enjoy your weekend. There are a lot of neighbourhood kids waiting for you to have a picnic,' I would have the most amazing two-hour bus ride. My head would be filled with the anticipation of all the fun things ahead.

Now I realise that I am the primary source that determines what makes me happy or sad and what makes me excited or nervous. It is the meaning I give to each event that occurs that determines how I feel about it, not the actual event.

If your life is going to be a purpose-driven one, you need to live and take action intentionally. As I say in my coaching programs, this process begins by creating a vision of how you want your life to be. By defining what your life's purpose is and who you are, you get to define what success is to you and what life is for you. We can call this your primary aim.

Understanding what your primary aim is helps you live your life intentionally. It helps you make conscious and thoughtful choices in your business and in your life, choices that are consistent and that factor in the things that are most important to you. It helps you set your priorities and see your business from the right perspective.

Once you've set and defined what your primary aim is, you can decide on how your business will contribute to this goal. You will create a business that is in line with your personal objectives and goals. Through this, your business is now also a way for you to get what you want from life. The moment you know what you count as success, you can streamline your actions towards achieving this goal.

A powerful tool developed by Simon Sinek called the Golden Circle can help you align your purpose with your business in an effective way. The Golden Circle finds order and predictability in human behaviour. Put simply, it helps us understand why we do what we do.

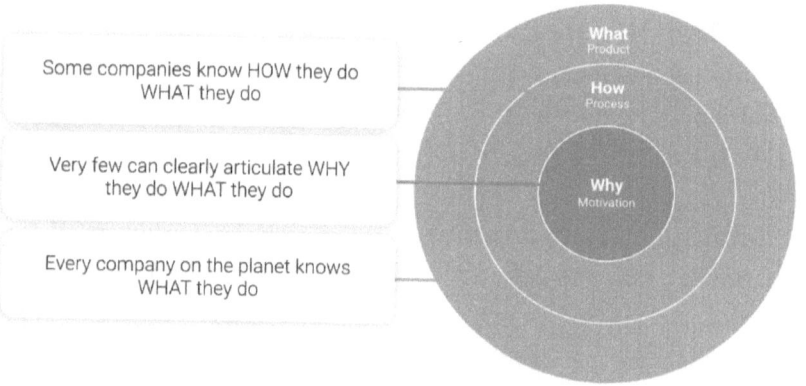

Graph inspired by Simon Sinek.

What: All companies know what they do or offer.

How: This explains how they do what they do and how they serve customers better.

Why: Only a few people can confidently state why they do what they do—their cause, belief, and purpose.

Most people and companies think and act from the *what* aspect to the *why*.

If Starbucks were like everyone else: 'We make great coffee. They are hand brewed, great to taste, and eco-friendly. Do you want one?'

How Starbucks actually communicates: 'In doing what we do, we believe in inspiring and nurturing the human spirit. We believe in creating the customer experience. We create an exceptional customer experience by making our products great to taste and eco-friendly. Also, we happen to make great coffee. Want to buy one?'

Starbucks does not just reverse the order; they start their message with *why* they do what they do. It states a purpose and belief without necessarily tethering it to what they do. What they do is no longer a reason to be a customer and buy coffee; it only shows the proof of the cause they believe in.

People don't buy what you do; they buy why you do it.

Organisations often apply the tangible and visible features of their company to explain why they and what they offer are better than other companies. Companies try to sell us their products, or their *what*. However, we mostly buy the *why*. When flipping the order, the *why* becomes the reason to buy, while the *what* is an example of this reason and belief.

Consumers and investors don't have a problem with Starbucks having so many distinct products in so many categories. However, Apple is not a major company today just because of *what* they do. They are, because of *why* they do it. Their products exemplify their cause, and all their actions are directed towards demonstrating their *why*.

In the course of competition, Starbucks competitors lost their *why*; they moved from being companies that had a cause and became companies that merely sold products. With that, price, quality, service, and features became their motivation. At this point, the companies stopped producing products and started producing commodities instead.

Your company does not need to be the best at producing what you produce. You just need it to either be good or be very good. Better or best only exists when comparing with other companies. If you don't understand the why, it is of no use to compare your product with others, even from the perspective of the customer.

If a customer feels motivated, as opposed to being bullied or manipulated, to buy your product, they will be able to state the reasons they think your product is better than others.

The cause and reason of your company or product is what inspires confidence and loyalty in the product, not the product itself.

Instead of asking '*What* should we do to compete?' we need to ask, '*Why* did we start doing *what* we're doing in the first place, and *what* can we do to bring our cause to life, considering all the technologies and market opportunities available today?'

To sum up, in order to enrol others into your vision, you need to begin with why. The more effective you are at aligning your why with your customers and employees, the faster you will be able to translate your visions into something tangible.

Distinction #3
Your Business Is the Way to More Life

I. Job, Career, and Mission

Do you view your current primary income source as your job, your career, or your mission? Different levels of thinking determine totally different outcomes.

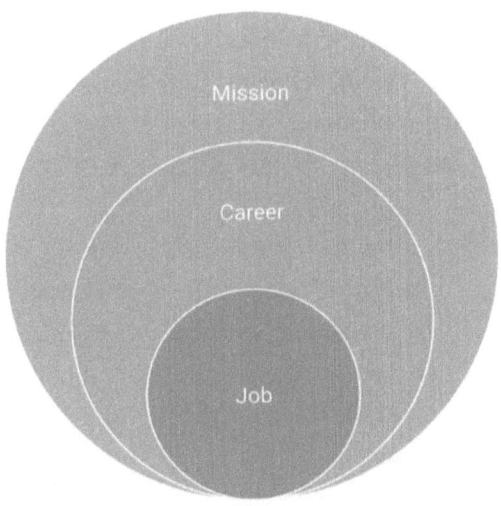

If you view your current job as just a basic income source to get you through the day and keep you busy and occupied, you will consider the people around you as just transactional relationships. If the business you started is just focused on creating a job for yourself, you will soon find it tiring; it would be better just working for someone else. This is because, in the job of owning and running a business, you need to work in so many different roles: marketing, human resource, and accounting. Sooner or later, you will burn out because of the sheer amount of tasks that you have assigned to yourself.

If you view your current income source as your career, you will have a much higher level of fulfilment. As you have committed yourself to the mastery of this field or profession, you cut out all other possibilities and pursue a singular pathway to success. That is where all the magic happens. Same for running a business. If you have committed to one field of business to master and serve, that is the unique DNA of your business. Every successful company always focuses on one successful product: Apple focuses on the MacBook, Starbucks focuses on coffee, and Nike focuses on sportswear. The singular focus represents who they are. It affects the way their customers perceive them. In other words, your customers may forget what exactly you do, but they will remember how you make them feel.

If you believe your current business is your mission, you have taken your game to a whole new level above just being a career. Everyone in your business is part of a mission that you have created. Every client is part of your mission to serve. You don't care how long it takes to serve them, because time disappears when you are doing something you feel fulfilled doing. How long does it take? Five minutes? Five hours? Five weeks? Time is an illusion. Once you find your mission and do what you love, there will be no time and space between you and fulfilling your mission. Every moment is spent creating and connecting, and your mission will draw a team of like-minded members to share and spread the mission to more people.

II. Business Is the Way to More Life

Financially wealthy people are those who have enough money coming in without having to work to finance their purpose in life. Now please realise that this definition presents a challenge to anyone who accepts it. To be financially wealthy, you must have a purpose for your life. In other words, without a purpose, you'll never know when you have enough money, and thus you can never be truly financially wealthy.

It isn't that having more money won't make you happy. To a point, it certainly can. But then it stops. For more money to continue to motivate, it depends on why you want more of it. It is often said that the end shouldn't justify the means, but be careful: when achieving fulfilment, any end you seek will only create fulfilment for you through the means it takes to achieve it. Wanting more money just for the sake of getting it won't bring the happiness you seek from it. Fulfilment emerges when you see a bigger picture which is more important than more money.

You may be thinking, *Personal fulfilment is all fine and well, but I have bills to pay!* You may also be wondering how exactly you can afford to live better when you're already working round the clock to keep the business in the clear.

Your business is *your way* to *more life*. What do I mean by *more life*? *More life* is being able to spend your time in different and enjoyable ways. It's about achieving the passions and dreams you have always had.

Consider this: If you were free to do anything right now, *what would you choose to do?* Would you remain here? Who would you choose to take some time out with?

Your business should contribute to you achieving your goals and visions. It should give you the financial ability that helps you enjoy *more life*. It is the asset that will sponsor your finances—even when you no longer work in it.

What is success to you? If you don't have any idea of what success is, how will you know what to strive towards, and how would you know if you are on the way to getting it?

For business owners who choose to adopt entrepreneurial thinking, success is in a business that 'works' and functions properly. A working business is a channel to *more life* for everybody it touches: the business owner, the business employees, the customers, and the community at large.

Through the entrepreneurial mindset, you have decided to establish not only a profitable business but one that is also easily marketable. Your biggest salary will not be from your wages or salaries but *from the day you choose to sell all or part of your business*. Investors will pay a lot for any business with steady and consistent profits. This is often called sweat equity, but in truth, it can be considered 'intelligence equity'—the value you add to a business by finding more efficient ways to do what should be done.

So what happens when you've created a business that can run in your absence? Congratulations! You've achieved a vehicle for *more life!*

True success to an entrepreneur is building a business that allows you to live the life that you want. It is building a business that allows you the money and freedom to do the things you really want to do. It helps you live your life as you want. True success lets you do what you love and work towards achieving your personal goals.

As you work on the business, you begin to see that it is a brilliant metaphor for working on your personal life—that at the core of it all, it is not just efficiency or effectiveness or more money, but the ability to create a better life for everyone the business touches, as well as you, the business owner.

Take a moment now to reflect on what you think of the following questions:

1. If you had the freedom to be doing anything right now, *what would you do?* Where would you be? Who would you like to spend your time with?
2. How are you going to apply the distinction of changing nothing to something in your personal life and business?

3. What is your *why*? Why do you want to establish the business?
4. How are you going to apply the 'why, how, what' sequence to your business mission statement?

> You put your experience into words, so it becomes thoughts and thoughts become ideas. Your ideas become actions, actions become habits, habits become your personality, and your personality becomes your destiny.

CHAPTER SIX

Principle 6
Empower Your Team

If you want to go fast, go alone. If you want to go far, go together.

African Proverb

After emerging from his palace one morning and on finding a beggar, a king asks, 'What do you want?'

The beggar laughs and says, 'You ask as though you can fulfil my desire!'

The king is offended, and he says, 'Of course, I can. What is it?'

The beggar warns, 'Think twice before you promise anything.'

Now the beggar was, in truth, the king's past-life master, who had told the king in their former life, 'I will come to try to wake you in our next life. This life you have missed, but I will come again to help you.'

The king, unaware that he was speaking to his old friend, insisted, 'I will fulfil anything you ask, for I am a very powerful king who can fulfil any desire.'

The beggar said, 'My desire is simple. Can you please fill up this begging bowl?'

'Of course!' the king said as he instructed his vizier to fill the man's begging bowl with money.

The vizier did as he was instructed, but as the money was poured into the bowl, it suddenly disappeared. So he kept on pouring, but as much as he poured, the bowl remained empty.

The news spread all across the kingdom, and a huge crowd soon gathered around the palace. The king's power and prestige were at stake, so he said to his vizier, 'If my kingdom is to be lost, I am ready to lose it, but I cannot be defeated by this beggar.' He continued to empty his wealth into the bowl.

Finally, as the crowd kept looking on, the king admitted defeat to the beggar. 'You are victorious, but before you go, fulfil my curiosity. What is the secret of this begging bowl?'

The beggar simply replied, 'There is no secret. It is simply made up of human desire.'

The begging bowl story shows us how a big challenge we face as people is ensuring that our lives do not end up like that beggar's bowl—a bottomless pit of want and desire making us keep searching for the next thing that will give us some happiness.

That is losing proposition.

Soon after I completed my MBA a few years ago, I developed anxiety for some months, as even though I had just accomplished a major milestone in life, I was confused about what I should do next. It was one of those moments when you feel like you have achieved a significant personal goal, but you feel the happiness only for a few days before you start to feel anxious about what needs to be done next. I seemed to have everything I wanted at that stage of my life, yet I felt like I was not connected to anyone.

I grew up in a remote town in South China. Neither of my parents had the opportunity to attend school, so earning an advanced degree was something I had always been extremely inspired to achieve since childhood. I decided to pursue an MBA not because I was looking for a corporate job but because I was focused on personal development, so I could have the capacity to further elevate my business development skills and help more clients. It was one of the most unforgettable experiences I have ever had. In the course of this program, I met so many wonderful people and course-mates in the program. We had a blast travelling around the United States and learning leading management strategies from masterminds in the field.

I broke down for a few months after the program. I believe that *'the more you have been given, the more you are obligated to give back'*. I was not sure where or how I could get started. The feeling was like if you were driving a fast car and wanted to drive it at its highest speed, but the speed limit on the road you're driving on is capped to fifty kilometres per hour. So you are stuck in second gear. You may feel powerless about what to do or how to change the situation.

I was reminded of the success stories from the twelve-step program widely used in Alcoholics Anonymous. If people successfully move through the first eleven steps but fail to embrace the twelfth, they often fall back into old habits. The final step asks them to help another alcoholic find recovery. The only way to feel fulfilled and content is by helping others achieve the same result. The concept behind this twelfth step is that if everything you strive to achieve is all about yourself, you will soon hit a brick wall or go back to your old routines and habits. We will do so much more for someone we care about than we will for even ourselves. What you can't create, you can't master. It is like solving a math problem: if you can't explain the solutions to others in the simplest language, you have not yet understood the problems or the solutions completely.

I decided to devote my Sunday to helping kids with special needs learn. One of my favourite students was Shaun. Half of his body was paralysed, so he needed to take pain relief medicine to reduce the pain due to the muscle cramps during our tutoring sessions. The medicine reduced his pain, but it also slowed down his brain capacity, limiting his ability to learn what was being taught. I taught him his year 12 math, and the main challenges I faced were having to slow down what I was teaching so he could catch up as well as trying to communicate with him properly.

It was a tremendous journey. I was a bit stressed out sometimes, not because of Shaun but because of myself and the difficulty I faced trying to get the results I thought he was capable of.

One day, while I was teaching Shaun, I asked myself, 'Lincoln, what if Shaun was not just your student but was also your team member? How would you go about this situation differently?'

With this one question, my entire thinking paradigm was shifted. I shifted my view on how Shaun should progress, and instead, I started to emphasise how I should view the way he progressed. As we were on the same team, if he didn't understand the concepts I shared with him, it meant we both wouldn't achieve the outcome together. If I went too fast at my own pace, all I just did was go for a walk by myself instead of leading the team.

Then it dawned on me that he was moving at the speed that he was supposed to be moving at. Remember, every time we are stressed about others, the stress we feel is actually caused by ourselves. We are overly focused on ourselves; we focus on what our expectations are and how they have not been met yet. Once we shift our focus from just ourselves to serving others, our entire world will change.

Try to read these couple of questions for a moment. Notice the different ways of asking questions between A and B:

A: What can I get out of this transaction?

B: How can I help this person at this intervention?

A: How can I make him work faster, to deliver the result I want?

B: How can I help him work faster, to achieve the results we want?

A: Why is he/she still not delivering the results I want?

B: What can I appreciate in his/her contribution to the results so far?

Can you see the difference? A is focused on achieving the goals himself, but in a dysfunctional way. The impact of this thinking is that while his goals can be attained in the short term, it may not be sustainable in the long run. Sooner or later, you will get exhausted, as you will find that no outcome will be sufficient enough to meet your expectations. People around you will avoid doing any work with you, not because they don't like you but because they can't keep up with the demands from you and because they do not feel connected to or understood by you. The entire relationship is based on transactions: 'If you do this for me, I will do this for you'.

On the other hand, the way B asks those questions is positive and empowering. B can achieve goals more efficiently compared with A. People would love to work with B, as they can sense B can help them achieve their set goals together. B is very positive; he can see the positive side of every occurrence. B may not be the most talented nor the most experienced in the group, but people in the team trust B, as B always contributes value to help the team advance to their goals together.

Once you shift your attention from yourself to other people, you have shifted your entire focus to creating a possibility. Life supports life, and our Creator made us to help each other. In this way, we can expand and improve our community.

The experience of teaching Shaun has taught me to be patient, compassionate, and most importantly, grateful. If you ever find yourself depressed or lost, help someone next to you. You will soon realise how lucky we are to have everything we have.

There is always more money to be made, there are always more university degrees to earn, and there are always bigger houses to buy. Our society has conditioned us to think that the more we have, the better off we are. In *David and Goliath*, Malcolm Gladwell examined the relationship between income and parenting. He argued what we all would expect to be true: it's hard to parent effectively when you are struggling to pay the bills. Money makes parenting easier, to a certain point. Then it stops making much of a difference. Children in wealthier families find it harder to learn the value of money, the meaning of work, and the joy and fulfilment that comes from making your own way in the world.

The Inverted U Curve

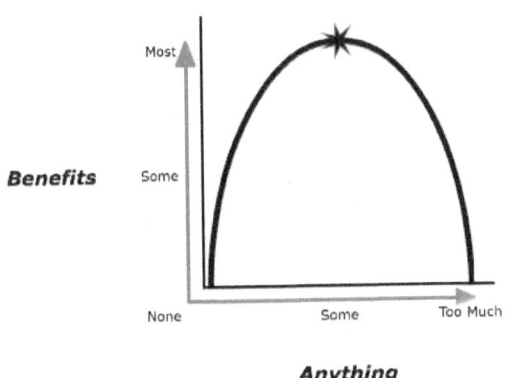

Scholars who research happiness suggest that more money stops making people happier after they exceed a $75,000 income level per year. There are stories of how parents with excess income end up raising troubled children. The answer? No. Research conducted in the United States shows that when you start making $75,000 annually, which is enough to handle life's necessities, having more money on top will not make you happier (Times, 2010). Why is this the case? Daniel Goleman, author of the well-renowned book *Emotional Intelligence*, quotes the Dalai Lama: 'Many people feel money is the source of a happy life. Money is necessary, useful—but more and more money does not bring happiness.' Money in itself is not a source of happiness. Our desire is like the beggar's bottomless bowl; there is never enough external stimulation that could truly satisfy us.

Who looks outside dreams; who looks inside awakens.

How can we ensure that we keep consistent standards for the goals we aim to achieve? This is the power of what a team does. The team we build around us keeps us accountable to the goals we set. The quality of our life is in a direct relationship with the quality of the team we build around us. Instead of figuring out how to improve our game of business, this chapter devotes itself directly to the core of the matter: empowering your team. The three distinctions I share in this chapter are going to enable you to build an empowering team in you and around you.

Distinction #1
How Situations Occur to Team = Team Performance

Take a moment to think about this: What if the business you start is just like a game? Now you are the captain of the team. You have to choose who is to be your team member and the mission you all come together to accomplish. The way you engage with your team members correlates directly with the outcome you are going to get. Who will be your team members in the business contest? Your team members extend over various scopes and aspects: your employees, your investors, your accountant, your lawyers, your suppliers, and yourself. Do you ever wonder why some teams perform so much better than others? What are the secret ingredients that exist behind the scenes to make the whole team stick together and move through the challenges through thick and thin? Under the same conditions, for example, in the exact same company franchise: 7-Eleven stores, McDonald's, and Burger King. The stores are fitted out exactly the same, and the procedures are exactly the same. So why is there such a big difference in the performance levels of these different stores? Shouldn't the store employees perform at a similar level?

No.

In every company or institution—as well as in your own personal life and career—there is a default future which you're sure will come into place. However, if you can enhance this future, better things can happen.

What is your *why*? What pushes you to do what you do? There a lot of ideas on human behaviour, but the truth is that whenever we do something, it is because it seems sensible or right to us. We always react to situations we find ourselves in based on how we perceive them. Your perception then combines your idea of the past and what you predict the future will be like.

All of us do things in light of how a situation appears to us.

There is a perfect link between the actions you take and how something appears to you. Consider if the coming weekend is going to be a holiday with family, and compare it with if the coming weekend is going to be full of housework. Which one would you be more excited about? If what will happen during the weekend is fun time with family, you will very much look forward to the coming weekend. However, if the coming weekend occurs to you as extra housecleaning work to be done all by yourself, you probably will not look forward to the weekend.

This is why it is often difficult to understand why some people do what they do. Until you see that person's world and consider how these situations appear to them, their actions may seem to you as irrational and not well thought out. Once you understand how things appear to other people, you start to understand their actions.

You should also note that how you perceive situations is affected by two things: your view of the immediate past and your anticipation of the near future.

A lot of attempts at change initiatives often fail in companies because the problems seem to be beyond what they can control. As such, change initiatives often reaffirm what exists already instead of making necessary changes. This results in a cycle like this:

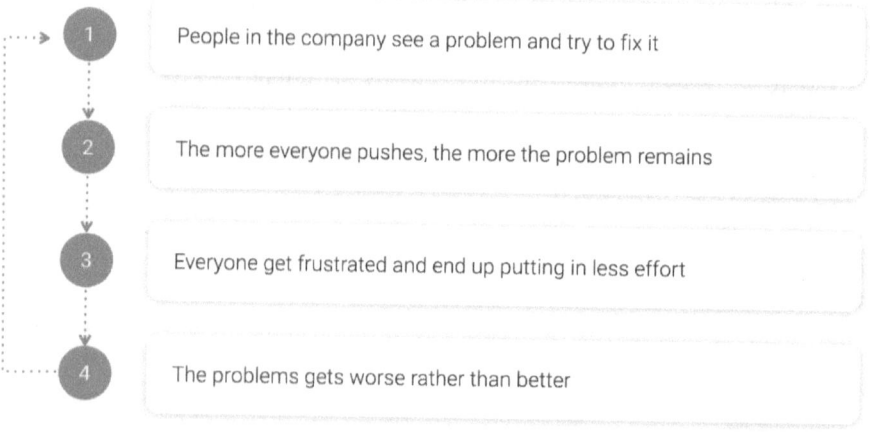

The major principle displayed here is 'Whatever you resist, persists'. The more you try to fight the challenges your company faces head-on, the more the problem attacks the organisation. The best way to move forward is to note what is currently stopping you from moving forward, which is your perception of how the situation is. Change this idea, and you can then face all your problems.

Let me give you a real challenge I faced many years ago:

When I had just started my financial consulting practice eight years ago, I always found it a challenge to share my business to my friends and potential clients. There was always a little voice in my head saying, *Stop being a pushy salesman, Lincoln. You are going to lose all your friends, and no one will ever like your products.* Marketing and sales seemed to me like a form of manipulation to get people's attention, which was far from my true intentions. My business was always capped due to my limited understanding of marketing and sales. This was until one day when I read a book called *Sell or Be Sold* by Grant Cardone. I realised I had gotten it all wrong. There is a quote in this book: 'Your ability to do well in life depends on your ability to sell others on the things in which you believe. Become so sold, so convinced, and so committed to your company, product and service that it would be a terrible thing for the buyer to do business anywhere else with any other product.' I realised that instead of worrying about whether or not others were willing to sign up for my service, I needed to look deep inside myself. Did I believe my service could actually provide better value than anyone else's in the market? I needed to strengthen my own belief first. It was my own duty and responsibility to convince myself first on why my service could provide value in the market. If I didn't even believe in my own products and services, why should others? The founder of Alibaba.com, Jack Ma, said it as well: 'Manipulation is sharing the things you don't believe while true selling is sharing the things you deeply believe in.' Whether or not others buy it is left to them, but you, the business owner, need to be 100 per cent convinced.

From that day onwards, I have altered my perception on marketing and sales. Marketing and sales no longer occur to me as manipulation. Instead, I believe it is simply just sharing what I believe with others. The marketing no longer worries me. I now have all the freedom to share myself without constraint on how others respond to what I share, because what I share is genuine and what I believe to be the best. In other words, marketing and sales occur to me differently than it did before, so I am able to perform better.

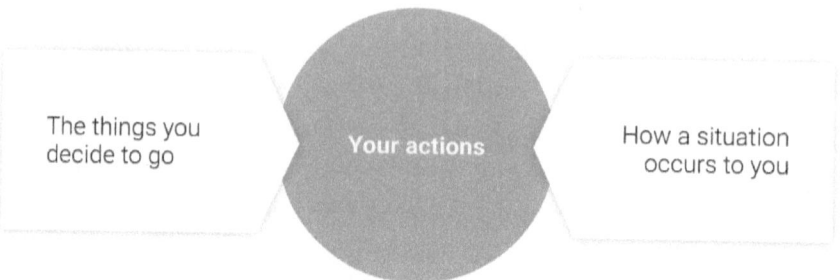

Back to the question we discussed at the beginning of distinction #1: Why is there so much difference in the franchise business performance even though the stores have similar structures and sell similar products?

The answer: the leaders make the business appear differently to the employees. In other words, some managers in the store make the work appear to the employees as another boring nine-to-five shift, while other successful managers make the store appear as a place for employees to learn, grow, and service others.

Your team performance = how the situation appears to them. It works every single time!

Distinction #2
Future-Based Language Elevates Team Performance

Think about this: One day, your boss asks you to go to his office. He says, 'Look, I think you made a small mistake on your previous quarterly performance report.' How would you respond? 'Sure, I will fix it,' I can hear you say.

However, what if your boss says, 'Look, I think you lied on the previous quarterly performance report'? How would you feel then? I can sense the temperature rising through your chest. Now note that the difference between the first conversation and the second is in just a few words.

The language you use to describe how you feel often determines how you address it. The language used to describe a challenge you are facing can determine whether or not you end up making changes for the better. Often the things that negatively affect our performance are more apparent in what is unsaid and assumed instead of what is stated openly within the organisation. To progress, you usually need to remove all the background problems and allow the use of better communication.

Language is a very complex and nuanced human phenomenon. It helps define what it is to be human. Language gives us a past and a bright future. It is what allows us to dream, to set goals, and to make plans for the future. Language is how our future is written, so it is only reasonable that if you want a different future, you should change the language you use.

Take a moment and think about an item you can't use language to describe. I bet you can't find any. Whatever you can see, hear, and feel, you use language to describe and create them. We call a table solid because we can put a book on top of it, so it is called solid. But in reality, the tabletop is not solid. Under a microscope, the tabletop is made of billions of atoms. It is not solid in the sense of how it is actually structured. However, we use language to create the reality. So the table is solid.

Note that language is not restricted to just the things that are said. It also includes:

- all spoken and written communication
- your body language, including facial expressions
- the tone of voice you talk with
- pictures, drawings, and other symbols

- the type of music you listen to
- how you dress and what your clothes say about you.

People use the languages they speak in two different ways:

It can be descriptive. Language can be used to describe past occurrences as well as what these issues were. Descriptive language is applicable when trying to look at the things of the past, such as past trends, and analysing everything that happened.

It can be future-based or generative. Language can be used to create and build a better, more attractive future, to shape a person's dreams and visions, and to remove the mental blinders that may exist already.

In their minds, most people have a default future in place. This is the future that they expect if everything happening today continues at the same pace:

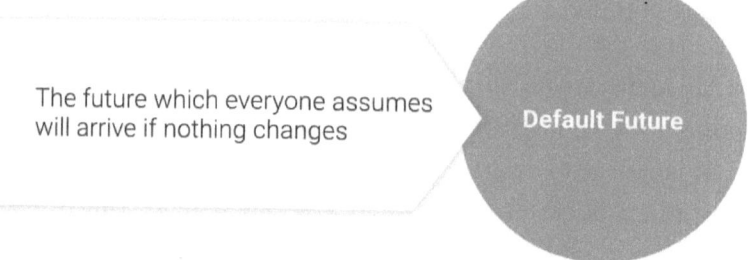

In simpler terms, the default future is an inferred view of the future based on what has happened in the past and what is happening today. It states that if everything stays constant and continues without changing today, this is the future that will be expected. Think about a team challenge you have at work or business right now, such as your employees not showing up for work or your supplier running late for a project. What language would you use to describe it? Most people would probably say something like 'The problem happened in the past. I will solve it just like I used to. He/she always acts in this way, there is not a lot I can do about it.'

Insanity is doing the same thing over and over again but expecting different results. We can't solve our problems with the same levels of thought that created them. That is why using the descriptive language to solve the challenge you face will not completely solve your challenge. The problem will show up again and again, as that is the default future.

For change to come into place, you need to make use of generative or future-based language, as opposed to descriptive language. With this, you change your default future into a better one which you have orchestrated yourself. If you can think up a future that is compelling, interesting, and inspiring for everyone that puts effort into making it come to pass, awesome things can and will happen.

Think about the same work and business you have. What if you change the language to future-based language? 'I understand the fact that my employee is not showing up for work and my supplier is running late on the project delivery. I am going to communicate with them and seek to understand how the situation came about in their own world. I am going to create an empowering work environment to let employees and suppliers have a trust community to perform their highest level.'

Can you see the difference made by using future-based language compared with descriptive language? Future-based language gives you the possibility of a new, better future.

Note that applying future-based language to create an interesting future may take a while. A lot of people need to be involved and contribute to the process. Ideas and creative thoughts need to be bounced around this group of people before a preferred future emerges in the mind. All this is not instantaneous and does not happen in a minute.

So how can you create a future that is inspirational and interesting? You are the author of your life; write your own script powerfully.

Distinction #3
Trade Your Expectation for Appreciation

I remember when I had just started out business in the earlier years. I needed to fly to China on a regular basis, as I needed to meet with business clients. I think that the best way to communicate with others is by meeting them face-to-face, not via text messages or emails. Modern technology has enabled us to send messages faster, but not more effectively. We get distracted more easily, but we feel more connected than ever before. So every year, I committed to seeing my distant clients face-to-face at least once so we could have the same level of communication and same understanding of the common goals we were creating.

My biggest challenge was not the twelve-hour flight itself. It was not having Internet during the twelve hours that made me upset. How was I going to survive during those hours? How would my business turn out after the twelve-hour flight? My mind started to get plagued by all kinds of fears.

One time, when I took a flight on the eve of Chinese New Year, there was a special announcement made saying that there was complimentary Wi-Fi access for all the guests. Everyone, including me, stood up, clapping for the airline for making such a generous gesture. It seemed like the best thing that could happen in life at that point. However, after the flight took off, within fifteen minutes, there was another announcement: 'Attention, all guests. Due to a technical difficulty, the Wi-Fi is not working at this time. We apologise for the inconvenience.' People around me started screaming and called the airline assistant to come over to explain why the Wi-Fi was not working. The lady sitting next to me was so disappointed she even started to write a complaint letter to the airline company. What was considered a miracle fifteen minutes earlier was now a disappointment, as expectations had not been met. What was considered a generous gift earlier was now seen as a disaster on the same scale as an airplane crash, at least to those of us it affected. It reminds me of how quickly people will react to a situation when their expectations are not met. This was despite the fact that people can drink coffee, enjoy movies, and read books at a 5,000-kilometre height while flying. Even birds can't do that. Once we focus on the expectations that have not been met, we forget what is actually great. When we focus on something, our energy will flow into those areas.

We have different preferences on things to be done. If people don't act the way we want them to act, our expectations are not met, so we end up suffering. What are the chances that people are going to meet our expectations all the time? What is the probability that the results are always going to turn out the way we want? It is almost impossible for that to happen. If we use our expectations to guide our daily decisions and feelings, we are doomed to suffer. Alternatively, if you can exchange your expectation for appreciation, there will be a noticeable shift in your life in a moment.

The feelings when you expect something as opposed to when you are appreciating something are pretty different. In one case, we feel owed, and in the other, we feel awed. Expectation is looking forward to what we hope to gain in the future. It has no room for the present moment. Appreciation is strictly about the here and now. We appreciate what we have and what is around us, which is a far more productive place to be.

This idea takes me back to my childhood, when my parents would repeat, 'Be grateful for what you have while still chasing everything you want.' It engrains a sense of gratitude and acceptance. This, of course, does not mean to stop working towards new goals, but instead it reminds us that when we shift our energy intently rather than split its focus, outcomes are naturally amplified.

When we start to appreciate what we have, we are able to move towards what we want, as what we have is more than enough to produce what we want. We begin to be resourceful. Your resources are not constrained by the money, time, and knowledge you hold. Your resource is your happiness with your team. Your resource is your joy when things do not go in your way. Your resource is that part of you that chooses not to settle; your resource is your hunger to keep creating value for your clients.

We engage in a simple spiritual act: loving thy neighbour as thyself. In business, if you don't do it, it will not work. What is business? It is finding ways to do more for others than everybody else. Pretty good religion, huh? It is finding ways to truly serve; it is caring enough to understand other people instead of just forcing your ideas on them because you are excited. It is taking the time to connect, to understand, and to appreciate. With that, you have been given the gifts of influence, because when people feel they are cared for, loved, and understood, they are open. But ultimately, this is about how you take what you envision and make it into something real. How do you take something invisible and convert it into something visible? We are all creators, as our Creator made us to create. Most people maintain, and most people manage resources. I invite you to remind your soul that you are a powerful creator. What is amazing is that if you can quickly convert your vision into reality, the faster it comes into existence, the less fear about failing you will have.

If our entire focus is on doing more than everybody else, on pushing through our fears, or on finding ways and appreciating all the opportunities that come up, what is more spiritual than that? Freedom is just a moment away—the time when you forget about what you will get and commit to appreciating everything you have.

Thinking time. Now I invite you to take a moment to reflect on the following questions:

1) How can I interact with people so they perceive the things that occur to them more meaningfully?
2) What processes, dialogues, or meetings can I put in place which would help my people feel like co-authors of the future instead of prisoners to the choices of other people?
3) What projects can I set up and involve people in which will help shape the company's future?
4) What view am I holding on my team's performance? How does my view impact my team's performance so they can perform better than they are performing now? What is a new view I can instil so we have space for a new possibility?
5) In what aspects of my business can I trade my expectation for appreciation right now?

Now It Is Your Time

I'm going to go out and do it and show myself that it's possible because the possibility is very contagious. If you prove yourself that something is possible in your life that you once thought was impossible, that's going to give you confidence throughout your entire life. And so one thing I do is, every single week, I try to do something that pops into my mind, 'Easier said than done' or 'That's impossible', and I go out there and do it and I show myself that is possible, so that helps me overcome fear.

Trent Shelton

You have made it; you have worked through six entire success principles. Now it is time to drive your business and finance to the next level. You are ready to write your brand-new chapter. Knowledge is not power; knowledge is potential power. If you are willing to give yourself an opportunity to put your experience into consistent action, you will find that the goals you envision are just around the corner. Like playing the football game instead of just sitting on the fence and wishing things would happen for you, you need to get into the court to make things happen. Nothing will get better until you get better. It will not get more comfortable; you need to get better. You have got what it takes, but it will take everything you've got. So commit to the game. It is your game, and now it is your time.

Your past stories are just a memory; they are not real unless you live in there. The only thing that stands between you and your goal is the false story you keep telling yourself about why you can't achieve them. You are the creator of your life, not just the manager of your circumstance. Most people manage their life; most people try to maintain the situation. I invite you to leave the past as passed and create a brand-new future from nothing. You are the author of your life, and you are in the brand-new chapter of your time. Time to write the script powerfully.

I hope this book unleashes your inner desire. I hope it inspires you to know that business is more than just making a living; building a business is a profound spiritual journey—to do more, become more, and give more.

I also hope this book lets you realise that your family needs you, your community needs you, and your friends need you. They need the powerful you, they need the authentic you, and they need the unleashed you.

I want you to know I'm deeply grateful to you and thankful for the privilege of spending this time with you. I know you are a unique human being, because most people don't pick up a book to improve their lives, much less read whole ones. If you read my words, you are now one of the few who do versus the many who talk. I also want you to know I sincerely hope this little book is going to be helpful to you on your journey to financial freedom and that you act on it and experience the blessing you deserve.

Please come back and reread it whenever you need a reminder of who you are and all you can indeed create in this life.

Remember, you are more than the moment. You are more than your business. You are more than any challenge you may encounter. You are the soul spirit essence; you can thrive in any economic condition. It has been my privilege to serve you; I look forward to coming across you sometime soon.

Further Reading

The following references served us greatly in our literature reviews for this project. Anticipating that a new generation of students interested in this emerging field will look for additional gateways to learning, we have included all that we deemed relevant. The author wishes to thank all the researchers and practitioners, both here and elsewhere, who generously provided their expertise and insight for this book and for our other efforts in inspiring the world to aspire for financial freedom and cultivating a better business community.

Ashton, M., and J. Currell (2017), *The MBA Mindset* (Melbourne: Major Street Publishing).
Cardone, G. (2013), *The 10x Rule* (Hoboken, NJ: Wiley).
Collins, J. (1994), *Built to Last* (New York: HarperCollins Publishers).
Collins, J. (2016), *Good to Great* (United States: Instaread).
Covey, S. (2005), *The 7 Habits of Highly Effective People* (London: Simon & Schuster).
Dalio, R. (2017), *Principles: Life and Work* (New York: Simon & Schuster).
DeMarco, M. (2011), *The Millionaire Fastlane* (New York: Viperion Publishing).
Ferrazzi, K., and T. Raz (2014), *Never Eat Alone* (New York: The Penguin Group).
Ferriss, T. (2007), *The 4-Hour Workweek* (United States: Vermilion, an imprint of Ebury Publishing).
Gerber, M. (2011), *The E-Myth Revisited* (New York: Harper Business).

Jeffers, S. (2011), *Feel the Fear and Do It Anyway* (New York: Simon & Schuster Audio).

Keller, G. (2013), *The One Thing* (London: Bard Press).

Kimbro, D., and N. Hill (1997), *Think and Grow Rich* (New York: Fawcett Columbine).

Kiyosaki, R. (1998), *Cashflow Quadrant* (New York: Plata Publishing).

Kiyosaki, R., S. Lechter, and R. Davidson (2001), *Rich Dad Poor Dad* (3rd edn, Prince Frederick, MD: Recorded Books).

Logan, D., and S. Zaffron (2013), *The Three Laws of Performance* (San Francisco, CA: Jossey-Bass).

Maxwell, J. (2002), *The 21 Irrefutable Laws of Leadership Workbook* (Nashville, TN: Thomas Nelson Publishers).

Ries, E. (2011), *The Lean Startup* (San Francisco: Crown Publishing Group).

Robbins, A. (2015), *Unlimited Power* (New York: Simon & Schuster).

Robbins, A. (2017), *Awaken the Giant Within* (New York: Simon & Schuster).

Robbins, A., and P. Mallouk (2016), *Unshakeable*.

Schwartz, D. (1988), *The Magic of Thinking Big* (Sydney: Simon & Schuster).

Grover, T. S. (2014), *Relentless* (New York: Simon & Schuster).

Sinek, S. (2009), *Start with Why* (New York: The Penguin Group).

Sinek, S. (2014), *Leaders Eat Last* (New York: The Penguin Group).

Stanley, T., and W. Danko (1996), *The Millionaire Next Door* (Sydney: Harper Business).

Tolle, E. (1997), *The Power of Now* (New York: Namaste Publishing).

Vaynerchuk, G. (2011), *The Thank You Economy* (New York: HarperCollins e-Books).

Vaynerchuk, G. (2017), *Crush It!* (New York: Harper Business).

About the author

Lincoln Pan is a successful entrepreneur, business consultant, and visiting lecturer for many elite business schools. He is the co-founder of three multimillion-dollar companies: LearnZillion, Cinch Advisers, and Mojo Property Group. He is also an active board member of many national not-for-profit organisations. Lincoln is extremely passionate about teaching, and his TEDx UWA seminar, 'Three Principles to Create Your Unshakeable Financial Future', amounts to one of the highest-rated workshops from participants.

Lincoln holds an MBA and attended an Executive Education program from Harvard Business School. He has received numerous awards, including the Excellence in Teaching award 2014, Education Entrepreneur of the Year 2015, and Young Business Professional of the Year 2018. Over the past ten years, Lincoln has successfully consulted and coached over three thousand individuals and businesses across seven countries. As CEO of LearnZillion, Lincoln leads a team of coaches, teachers, and researchers whose mission is to help people create and enjoy an extraordinary life. He supports both companies and individuals to cultivate a resilient financial structure and empowers business owners and entrepreneurs to align their passion with long-term economic sustainability strategically. The experience he has gained from working as both a business owner and financial adviser has enabled him to unleash individual financial performance through innovative financial coaching and authentic strategic interventions.

Index

A

accounting xix, 33, 44, 52, 95
adolescence 53-4, 56
artists 4, 42-3, 45-7, 49-51, 58-9

B

business development 16, 55, 74
business development stages 53
business owners xxiii, xxvi, xxix, 4-5, 10, 15, 34, 48-51, 53, 55-7, 59, 62-3, 66, 97-8, 109, 124
business structure 13, 53, 58

C

cash flow 12, 15-16, 19, 22, 55
client journey map (CJM) 68

D

design thinking viii, 63-6, 68-9, 71-3, 77-8

E

employment xix, 9, 11-15, 21
entrepreneurs ix, xii, 37, 46, 49, 56, 60, 62, 98, 123-4
expansion 37, 53, 55-6, 59

F

financial freedom viii, x, xx, xxiv-xxvi, 7, 19, 21, 27, 37, 51, 120-1
financial goals 6, 79, 90
financial success x, 12, 36-7, 50-1

G

Golden Circle 92

H

human resources 48, 52, 95

I

ideating stage 69-70
imagination 85-6
income paradigms 9, 11-12, 15-17
    characteristics 11
income streams 8-9, 14-17
    levels of 15-16
infancy stage 53-7, 59
investment xix, 9, 12-13, 17-20, 22, 43, 63, 70
    property 21-2
    share 21
investors xxvii, 10-11, 15, 31, 82, 93, 98, 106

K

Kiyosaki, Robert T. 9
knowledge base xxvii

L

language
    descriptive 112-13
    future-based 113

M

Ma, Jack 63, 109
managers 46-7, 49, 56, 58-60, 72, 74, 110, 120
marketing 16, 31, 44, 48, 52, 56, 66, 84, 95, 109-10
marketplace 18-21, 44
mastery
    artist 49
    business 49
    technical skills 49
maturity stage 53-5, 57-9
minimum viable product (MVP) 71-2

O

operators 46, 48-51, 66

P

Pareto principle 32
passion 5, 11, 49-50, 67, 73-8, 97, 124
personal development xix, 64, 102
prototypes 70

S

Sinek, Simon 92
Steve Jobs 17, 35, 47

T

team performance 106, 110, 117
technicians 46, 48-9, 51, 55-6, 58-60
testimonials 86-7
three purpose circles (TPC) 72, 74, 77